PLANT PROTECTION
IN THE GARDEN

A guide to pest, disease and weed control
in garden and home

Edited by:

G. W. IVENS, J. STUBBS

and the Scientific Staff of
The Royal Horticultural Society, Wisley

THE BRITISH CROP PROTECTION COUNCIL

THE ROYAL HORTICULTURAL SOCIETY

British Library Cataloguing in Publication Data

Plant Protection in the Garden.
1. Gardens. Plants. Pests, diseases and weeds. Control measures.
I. Ivens, G. W.   II. Stubbs, J.   III. Royal Horticultural Society
IIII. British Crop Protection Council
635'.049

ISBN 0-948404-39-6

Design by Gordon Rushmer Ltd. Liss, Hants.
Phototypeset by Applegraphics Limited, Winchester
Printed in Great Britain by Brown & Son (Ringwood) Ltd.

Foreword

The aim of all gardeners is to cultivate strong, healthy plants whether for ornament or for food, and in order to do this successfully, they need to be as free as possible of pests and diseases. Equally it is important that cultivated plants are not in competition with weeds for the available food and water.

If ideal cultural conditions are provided it is usually possible to keep the weed populations low by hand weeding or hoeing; and an attack by pests and diseases may only cause relative minor difficulties if the plants are maintained in robust and vigorous growth. But even under optimum conditions for the plants concerned, pests and diseases may still be a problem; and ideal conditions for cultivated plants are also greatly appreciated by many weeds. In some instances it may be practical to use biological control to combat certain pests but for the amateur gardener it is not easy to achieve the balance required and it may then be necessary to resort to using chemical methods of control.

In a society now very conscious of the importance of environmental issues it is vital that, in any of man's activities that affect the natural world, we act responsibly and are fully aware of the impact that our actions may have upon it. The sometimes careless and indiscriminate use of chemicals in agriculture and horticulture has contributed to our awareness of the difficulties that can and do occur and it is clear that a reasoned system of control in the use of chemicals is essential.

It is equally important, however, to recognise that we depend on agriculture and horticulture for our very existence. Cultivation of crops, whether on a commercial scale or in the garden, means that, by growing large numbers of one species or cultivar in a limited area, we are creating very favourable conditions in which pests, diseases and weeds can thrive, and if left uncontrolled, they will seriously damage or destroy the plants. So the sensible and safe use of chemicals, in the smallest quantities possible and integrated, where practical, with biological control, may be necessary.

There is a very large choice of chemicals now available for amateurs to help them combat weeds, pests and diseases in the garden – but it is by no means easy to select the appropriate product to overcome the particular problem that has arisen.

Plant Protection in the Garden has been jointly produced by the British Crop Protection Council and the Royal Horticultural Society with just this aim. It provides accurate information on the products available and gives the guidance essential to gardeners when faced with the bewildering range of chemicals marketed for control of pests, diseases and weeds.

All the products listed are registered under the control of Pesticides Regulations (1986) as approved for garden use and advice is also provided on how best to apply the chemical concerned and to achieve effective control without damage to people, the environment or the plants requiring protection.

The authoritative guidance to the use of chemicals provided in this book has long been needed, not only by amateur gardeners, but by personnel at nurseries and garden centres who are frequently called upon to give advice on garden chemicals.

This excellent publication has been very carefully researched and the data compiled to the highest degree of accuracy possible and those who use *Plant Protection in the Garden* can be confident that, whatever level of control is required, it will provide them with the information needed to select the product most appropriate to their needs.

Christopher D. Brickell
Director General
The Royal Horticultural Society, London

Contents list

Plant Protection in The Garden

Disclaimer

Every effort has been made to ensure that all the information in this book is correct at the time of going to press, but the Editors and the publishers do not accept any liability for any error or omission in the content, or for any loss, damage or any other accident arising from the use of the products listed herein. Omission of a product does not necessarily mean that it is not approved and available for use.

Notwithstanding any statement appearing in the book, it is essential that the approved product label should be read carefully and any instructions it contains regarding handling, storage, use and disposal should be carefully followed.

Control of Pesticides Regulations 1986

Under the Food and Environment Protection Act 1985 strict controls were introduced over all aspects of the supply, storage and use of pesticide chemicals in Britain, as specified in the Control of Pesticides Regulations 1986. All products classed as pesticides and intended for use in the garden and around the home must be registered specifically for such uses. Registration involves official approval of the product label submitted by the supplier together with the issuing of a registered number. Products for use in the garden normally have a number issued by the Ministry of Agriculture, Fisheries and Food (MAFF Number), many of those for use in and around the home are registered with the Health and Safety Executive and have HSE Numbers. Products must be used in accordance with the label instructions and it is an offence to use them other than for the purposes specified.

It is no longer permissible for products registered for professional use in agriculture, horticulture or forestry to be used in the home garden. It is also illegal for any approved pesticide to be supplied in any but the original container. Thus the home gardener may no longer legally obtain for his own use small quantities of any pesticide which was supplied to a nurseryman or garden centre in a larger container.

Purpose of the book and contents

The aim of all gardeners is to grow healthy, vigorous, pest and disease-free plants and to keep down the weeds which constantly threaten to invade the flower beds, fruit and vegetable plantings and lawns. Whilst many weeds can be removed by hand-weeding or hoeing most pests and diseases can only be adequately controlled with the aid of chemicals. Ideally, the use of chemicals should be kept to the effective minimum and, whenever possible, cultural and biological control measures should be combined with chemicals in an integrated system of plant protection. In this way damage to plants, to wildlife and the environment can be avoided.

The purpose of this book is to provide advice on how chemicals can be used safely to protect garden plants and to control household pests. More than 350 chemical products are available for use in combatting pests, diseases and weeds in the garden or around the home and for regulating plant growth. This faces the average gardener or householder with a confusing choice. Even for garden centres and others called upon to give advice it is often difficult to know what products are appropriate and available for use in a particular situation. Our aim is thus to ease the task of deciding what chemicals can be used to deal with any of the problems of plant protection which may arise.

This is done by providing a summary of the recommendations for use provided by the suppliers of chemical products in the form of labels or other advisory literature. The information is arranged in such a way that the products suitable for use against a particular type of disease, pest or weed in a particular situation can be readily identified.

A list of all the pesticide products approved under the Control of Pesticides Regulations is published annually, together with information on the active ingredients, in a joint MAFF/HSE publication, the current edition being *Pesticides 1990*. However, this gives no information on the uses for which the products are approved and many of the products listed are not currently available. The present book is intended to fill this gap by concentrating on the products which are to be found on sale and giving details of the purposes for which their use is permitted.

To be included in this book products subject to the Pesticide Regulations must have official approval, information on the approved uses must have been provided by the supplier and the product must be expected to be available on the market in 1990. We have attempted to provide as complete a coverage as possible. There may, however, be some registered products on the market which have not been included, either because we were not aware of them or because no information about them was received. No discrimination against any such products is intended.

The book is made up of two main parts, a 'Guide to pest, disease and weed control' and 'Chemicals available for use'. Each part is divided into several sections dealing with the major areas in which chemicals may have uses. These areas are:
- Crops (a general term covering fruit, vegetables, flowers and ornamentals grown outside)
- Lawns

- Greenhouses
- Houseplants
- Uncropped ground (paths, drives, etc.)
- General chemicals, including slug and snail control, domestic insecticides, bird and animal repellents and rat and mouse killers
- Miscellaneous products, including rooting hormones, growth retardants, fruit setting agents and non-chemical insect control.

The 'Guide to pest, disease and weed control' gives general advice on how to deal with the problems that occur in different situations in the home and garden. It is followed by 'Chemicals available for use' which consists of profiles of the individual chemicals or mixtures of active ingredients. Chemicals form part of, but rarely the complete, answer to many problems of plant protection and both parts of the book should be consulted to obtain the best solutions to problems.

The profiles are numbered and it is these numbers which are referred to in the index of product names at the back of the book. As shown in the index to sections on page 46, the sections are subdivided according to whether the chemicals are used as insecticides, fungicides or weed and moss killers, etc. Within each sub-section the profiles are arranged in alphabetical order of the names of the chemicals.

Profiles consist firstly of the name(s) of the active ingredient(s). Where the products contain important non-pesticide ingredients in addition to the active chemical they are listed separately. Thus mosskillers formulated together with fertilisers for use on lawns are separate from those without fertiliser.

A brief description of the nature and type of activity of the active ingredient(s) is given below the name of the chemical. This is followed by a cross-reference to other sections in those cases where products have uses in more than one field. Simazine, for example, may be used as a weedkiller in roses (a crop) as well as for total vegetation control on non-crop areas.

Below the cross-reference, details of the products are given in the following form:

(1)	(2)	(3)	(4)
Murphy Weedex	Fisons	WP	02352

(1) Product name
(2) Supplier (see Appendix for full name and address)
(3) Formulation code (see list of abbreviations following)
(4) MAFF Number (in form Hxxxx for HSE numbers)

followed by a section on the uses for which the products are recommended. Where there are several products based on the same active ingredient(s) and the recommended uses vary, the different uses are numbered in square brackets, the numbers corresponding to the product numbers.

The subsequent paragraph gives details of how to obtain successful results with the treatment and of any precautions needed to avoid undesirable effects on the plants treated or on other garden plants. A final paragraph is included where special precautions are needed to avoid undesirable chemical residues or any risk of injury to humans, pets, birds, fish, beneficial insects or wildlife generally.

List of abbreviations (formulation codes)

AE   Aerosol spray
AL   Other liquids to be applied undiluted
CB   Bait concentrate
CR   Crystals
DP   Dustable powder
DS   Powder for seed treatment
EC   Emulsifiable concentrate
FU   Fumigant
GR   Granules
GS   Grease
IM   Impregnated material
LA   Lacquer
LB   Liquid bait
LI   Liquid, unspecified
PA   Paste
PT   Pellets
RB   Ready-to-use bait
RH   Ready-to-use spray in hand-operated sprayer
SC   Suspension concentrate
SG   Water soluble granules
SL   Water soluble concentrate
SP   Water soluble powder
VP   Vapour releasing product
WP   Wettable powder
WX   Wax
XX   Other formulations

How to use the book

The book may be used in two ways to find possible answers to any particular pest, disease or weed problem. Firstly, by referring to the section of the Guide dealing with the appropriate type of plant and problem. For example, if the problem is one of rust on roses, the section of the Guide on 'Ornamentals' under 'Disease control' (pages 13–16) will be found to include suggestions for various chemical or other treatments which may be used to obtain control. By consulting the relevant profiles on these chemicals the products containing them can be readily identified.

The alternative is to look through the profiles in the 'Crop Fungicide' section (AB) to find which products are listed for control of the particular combination of disease and crop of interest. The latter approach is likely to show up a larger number of possible treatments, the former the ones which are most commonly employed.

When a product has been selected on the basis of the information presented here it must always be confirmed by referring to the approved product label as this provides the ultimate authority regarding the uses which have been officially approved.

An index of product names is provided at the end of the book which makes it easy to determine their active ingredients. An index of active ingredients is also provided.

Precautions with pesticides

Pesticides marketed for use in the garden and around the home are specially formulated, packed and labelled for the amateur user. It is recognised that the home gardener or householder is unlikely to have access to the range of protective clothing needed to use safely the formulations supplied to farmers, growers and other professional users of pesticide chemicals. Thus, before official approval for a home garden formulation is granted it must be accepted that it can be applied safely without the need for special protective clothing, that it presents no hazards to children, pets or wildlife which might be accidentally exposed to it and that surplus chemical can be disposed of safely through normal household waste disposal systems.

When a product receives approval any precautions needed for its safe use are laid down and such precautions must appear on the label. All products can be used safely provided that the instructions are followed carefully and any specified safety precautions taken. For the great majority of garden chemicals and domestic pesticides the precautions are common-sense measures which apply equally to the handling of any type of chemical. The following should be regarded as a basic minimum even when not specified on the label:

BEFORE USE
- Store in a safe place out of reach of children.
- Keep in original container, tightly closed in a safe place.

DURING USE
- Do not breathe spray mist, dust or fumes.
- Keep off skin; wash off splashes.
- Wash hands and exposed skin after use.
- Keep away from food, drink and animal feeding stuffs.
- Avoid drift onto other garden plants.
- Keep away from children, pets, fish, etc.
- Keep pets off treated areas until spray has dried.

AFTER USE
- Do not store surplus spray solution.
- Wash out empty container thoroughly and dispose of safely.
- Empty sachets completely and dispose of safely.
- Do not re-use empty container.
- Wash out spraying equipment thoroughly before and after use.

The standard precautions are not repeated under each profile but, in cases where an extra degree of care is necessary, this is indicated. For example, where insecticide products are classed as 'dangerous', 'very dangerous' or 'extremely dangerous' to fish (rather than 'harmful') a statement to this effect is included. Similarly, whereas most insecticides present some degree of hazard to bees, mention of this is only made where there is a special danger to bees.

For products used on fruit and vegetable crops grown for human (or animal) consumption it may be necessary to allow a period after the last application to avoid any danger of residues remaining in the produce after harvest. Any requirement for such a 'harvest interval' is included in the profiles as a special precaution.

Application of Chemicals

In applying pesticide chemicals the primary aim is to cover the target evenly with the recommended dose of chemical. The equipment needed to achieve this depends on the way in which the chemical has been formulated.

Sprays

The traditional garden pesticide formulation is a liquid concentrate intended to be mixed with water and applied as a spray. The concentrate may be a solution in water, a solution in organic solvents with added emulsifier (emulsifiable concentrate), or a suspension concentrate. With all these the required volume must be measured out and mixed with a measured volume of water to obtain the correct dilution. The procedure is made easier with many products by packaging in ready measured sachets or the use of self-measuring bottles. Some solid formulations, such as wettable powders, water soluble powders or soluble grains, are also intended for spray application and the need to weigh out small quantities of solid material may also be avoided by the use of sachets.

Many types of sprayer are available and selection of the most suitable type depends to a large extent on the size of the area to be treated. For house plants and small greenhouses simple atomisers may be adequate, for larger scale treatment pressure sprayers will usually be needed. In situations where a fine spray is not necessary, for example on lawn weeds or for moss control on hard surfaces, application from a watering can equipped with a fine rose or one of the sprinkler bar attachments available will give good results. In all cases where spray liquid is applied from a rechargeable sprayer or other applicator it is essential to wash the equipment thoroughly before and after using it and the use of a separate applicator kept solely for herbicides is strongly recommended.

For a number of pesticides used on greenhouse and house plants, and for the majority of the products used in the home, the ready-to-use aerosol spray can provide a convenient method of application. Aerosol sprayers produce a mist of very fine droplets and are intended for use either as space sprays in enclosed areas or as a light application to surfaces from a distance of about 30 cm (12 in.). An increasing number of products are also appearing in ready-to-use, non-rechargeable, trigger operated spray guns, ideal for use on small areas or for spot treatment.

Dusts and granules

Most products formulated as dusts are supplied in puffer packs from which they are easily distributed. Granular formulations can sometimes be scattered satisfactorily by hand but, for even distribution of granular lawn treatments, including lawn sands, one of the proprietary spreaders available will give better results. In addition to the standard type of wheeled spreader, a new type of hand-held, ready-to-use applicator which incorporates a spout leading to a distributor plate held some distance above the lawn, allows the treatment of a strip 60 cm (24 in.) wide.

Fumigants and vapour releasing materials

The main use of fumigants is for the control of pests and diseases in the greenhouse. Such formulations are particularly suitable for controlling such pests as red spider mite and whitefly. The commonest formulation is the smoke cone. These burn for 10–15 seconds on lighting and fill the greenhouse with smoke, which penetrates into all the corners and crevices. In using such cones it is necessary first to close all greenhouse vents and, after lighting the cones, to keep the house closed for at least four hours. The house should be left as soon as the cone has been lit and it must be ventilated thoroughly for one hour before re-entry.

Dichlorvos is a volatile insecticide useful for controlling insects in enclosed spaces. It is commonly incorporated into strips of plastic designed to be suspended in rooms, greenhouses, etc. The size of the strip varies according to whether it is intended for use in large (living room), medium (kitchen) or small (cupboard, wardrobe) spaces.

Formulations for special purposes

Various formulations are produced for applying chemicals onto specific sites. These include:

- paint-on lacquer – persistent insecticide treatments for use in the home
- paint-on gel – for spot treatment with a non-selective weedkiller
- wipe-on products – such as fly-pens and weed-pencils
- treated materials – such as grease bands, brassica collars and 'spikes' or tablets impregnated with a systemic, root-absorbed insecticide for insertion into the growing medium alongside pot plants.

Disposal of residues

Before any pesticide can be approved for garden use the authorities have to be satisfied that no special problems are likely to arise in the disposal of surplus chemical. However, users of chemicals are under an obligation to protect the environment and to avoid pollution so that it is necessary to adopt certain standard precautions, as follows:

- When diluting concentrated products only mix up enough for the job in hand.
- Do not store any surplus diluted spray, other than that in ready-to-use containers. Diluted sprays are likely to deteriorate rapidly.
- If any surplus liquid remains after the completion of spraying distribute it over an unsurfaced path or drive or on waste ground not intended for cropping for at least 12 months.
- Dispose of washings in the same way as above.
- Do not dispose of surplus chemical spray or washings where they are likely to enter ditches, watercourses or ponds.
- For the disposal of small quantities of unwanted chemical in concentrated form leave it in the container, firmly closed, wrap in newspaper and place in the dustbin. Empty containers should be disposed of in the same way.
- For the disposal of larger quantities of pesticide which cannot be used for the purpose intended or for old containers found to contain products no longer permitted to be used or of doubtful contents, the local waste collection authority or, if known, the manufacturer should be consulted for advice.

Plant Protection in The Garden

GUIDE TO PEST, DISEASE AND WEED CONTROL

Crop chemicals

Pest control – general

Ants

Although these social insects do not directly injure plants they can cause much indirect damage. Ants tunnelling in the soil around growing plants can upset the root action causing the plants to wilt and die. They also 'farm' aphids, mealybugs and scale insects and so encourage the spread of these other pests. On lawns the mounds of soil thrown up over ant nests spoil the appearance of the sward and also interfere with mowing. They may be controlled with borax and a wide range of general purpose insecticides, such as carbaryl, gamma-HCH, permethrin, phoxim, pirimiphos-methyl and pyrethrum.

Aphids

Sap-feeding insects common as pests of fruit crops, vegetables and ornamental plants. Although commonly referred to as greenfly and blackfly, their colour ranges from white, through various shades of yellow, orange, red, brown and blue to black.

Feeding on young tissues they weaken and distort the plant growth. In addition they excrete copious quantities of sugary honeydew which usually becomes infested with unsightly sooty moulds. Aphids also transmit virus diseases from diseased to healthy plants. Throughout the spring and summer female aphids breed asexually, giving birth to live young which mature in about a week, thus giving dramatically fast increases in population.

Some degree of natural control of aphids is provided by predatory insects , such as ladybirds, hover fly larvae and lacewings. Garden birds also feed on aphids. Insecticides, however, are normally needed to give an adequate degree of control and for this purpose one can use either systemic chemicals, such as dimethoate or heptenophos, or contact sprays, such as fenitrothion, gamma-HCH, malathion, permethrin, pirimicarb, pirimiphos-methyl, pyrethrum or rotenone (derris). Products based on pirimicarb are of special interest since this insecticide, whilst highly active against aphids, has no ill effects on their natural predators or on bees or other beneficial insects.

Capsid bugs

Small, active, sap-feeding insects which attack the young growth of a wide range of plants. They pierce the plant tissues with their stylets, injecting saliva and then feeding on the plant sap. Their saliva kills the surrounding plant tissue, producing small, ragged holes in the leaves. Later the affected leaves develop a characteristic tattered appearance. Buds and shoots may

2

be killed and the developing flowers deformed, while injury to apples often shows as humps or other irregularities on the developing fruit.

Clearing away debris from the soil surface gives some control of overwintering adults and tar oil winter washes deal with the overwintering eggs on fruit trees and bushes. These measures, however, need to be reinforced by spray applications of chemicals, such as dimethoate, fenitrothion, gamma-HCH or pirimiphos-methyl, at the first signs of damage in spring or early summer.

Cutworms

These are the caterpillars of several species of moth which live in the soil and feed on the surface at night, attacking plants at ground level and often eating right through the stems, causing wilting and death of the plants. Young lettuce and brassicas are especially vulnerable but cutworms also feed on carrots, celery, brassicas and potatoes. Strawberries, too, may be attacked, as can a wide variety of ornamental herbaceous species and young trees and shrubs.

Some measure of control can be obtained by cultivating the soil during winter to expose the caterpillars to predators and the weather. Keeping the ground weed-free also helps to reduce the population. Protect young plants by applying a soil insecticide such as bromophos, gamma-HCH, phoxim or pirimiphos-methyl.

Leaf miners

Damage by these pests shows up either as sinuous white lines or as blistered blotches on the leaves. The damage is caused by the small larvae of moths, flies, sawflies or beetles which burrow into the leaf tissues and may occur in a wide range of shrubs, trees and herbaceous plants. Although they disfigure the foliage these pests usually have little effect on plant growth. The carnation leaf miner, however, which attacks the leaves and stems of carnations, pinks and sweet williams, can cause wilting and death of the plant. If only a few leaves are affected the best approach may be simply to pick off the damaged leaves. More serious attacks can be dealt with by applying an insecticide such as gamma-HCH or pirimiphos-methyl.

Mites

These tiny pests are only just visible to the naked eye and differ from insects in having four pairs of legs instead of three. Some species are predators or scavengers but others feed on living plant tissues. Some, such as the blackcurrant gall mite, attack only one specific host plant. Others, including red spider mites, are much less selective and can cause damage to a very wide range of indoor and outdoor plants. Red spider mite shows up as localized yellow speckling on the upper side of infested leaves caused by the pests feeding on the underside. The foliage becomes increasingly discoloured and may develop a bronze tinge before falling prematurely. Greenhouse and indoor plants infested with red spider mites

often become festooned with fine silky webbing. Control requires repeated application of an insecticide such as dimethoate, malathion, pirimiphos-methyl or rotenone (derris).

Scale insects

These sap-sucking insects are easy to recognize because of their shell-like covering and static feeding position. Females lay hundreds of eggs under waxy scales or coverings of white, waxy wool. Nymphs (crawlers) hatch from the eggs and move around before settling down to feed and complete their development. Like aphids, scale insects excrete sticky honeydew which soon becomes covered with unsightly sooty mould growth.

One method of control is to lightly scrape or brush off the adult scales and it is recommended that newly acquired plants should be carefully examined and any scales removed before putting them into the greenhouse or bringing them into the home. Heavy infestations can be dealt with by the application of malathion or pirimiphos-methyl. This treatment is most effective against the crawler stage so that outdoor plants are best treated in late spring or early summer, the main period for crawler activity. In heated greenhouses and in the home, however, crawlers may hatch at any time so that plants in these situations should be checked regularly, using a hand lens, to assess when to spray. An alternative approach on grapevines, bush fruits and apples is to use dormant season winter washes to control the immature or overwintering scales.

Thrips

Small winged insects, commonly called thunder flies, which are sap feeders on leaves, flowers and buds. They produce a characteristic light mottling or silvering and can cause the plant growth to be deformed. Glasshouse thrips also excrete red and brown liquid globules. They attack onions, brassicas, tomatoes, peas and broad beans, together with a wide variety of ornamental plants, including roses, privet and gladioli. Thrip infestations in the greenhouse are favoured by under-watering and overheating, so that regular watering and the maintenance of a cooler and more humid atmosphere are to be recommended.

Thrips are controlled by repeat applications of such insecticides as dimethoate, gamma-HCH, malathion, permethrin or pirimiphos-methyl.

Weevils

Both the adults and larvae of this type of beetle attack cultivated plants. The adults generally feed on the leaves, cutting holes in the lamina or gnawing notches in the margins. They may also bite through the leaf petioles and flower stalks and gnaw the bark of young shoots. Since they are nocturnal feeders and hide under surface debris or in the soil during the day they are rarely seen at work. The legless larvae have brown heads and fat, curved white bodies, living in the soil and feeding on the roots of a wide range of plants. The root damage reduces growth and in extreme cases can lead to wilting and death of the affected plants.

Applying an insecticide containing gamma-HCH, permethrin or pirimiphos-methyl to the plant foliage gives some control of the adult weevils but a better approach is to dust the surrounding soil with an insecticidal powder. Plants can be protected from larval attack by working a soil insecticide, such as gamma-HCH or pirimiphos-methyl into the upper layers of the soil. Protection of pot plants can be obtained by incorporating insecticide into the compost when potting up.

Pest control – ornamentals
(including roses, shrubs and flowers)

Adelgids
These are a type of woolly aphid which attack conifers. They are sap-feeders and may be found on the young shoots where they are easy to spot because of their white, waxy, woolly covering. They do not usually have serious effects on mature trees but can cause serious damage to young specimens. The spruce-gall adelgid (also known as the pineapple gall woolly aphid) causes the production of galls at the branch tips which look like small pineapples. It may be controlled by application of the liquid formulation of bromophos but it is important to kill the insects before the galls are initiated in early spring, which means spraying before the needles emerge.

Box sucker
A sap-feeding insect which infests the shoot tips and causes the young leaves to turn inwards and form a cabbage-like gall. Cut off and destroy any infested shoot tips and spray with dimethoate in April or May to deal with any nymphs which may be present.

Broom gall mites
The scales of buds infested with this pest become swollen and give the appearance of a tiny green rose. Insecticides are not effective and control is best achieved by picking off and destroying the galls.

Cabbage rootfly
The white maggots of this pest tunnel into the roots of aubrietia, stocks and wallflowers, causing them to wilt in dry weather. Established plants usually survive, though their growth is reduced. Young seedlings, however, may be killed. Attacks can be prevented by applying a soil acting insecticide, such as bromophos, gamma-HCH, phoxim or pirimiphos-methyl over the seed drill and around newly planted seedlings.

Caterpillars
Caterpillars of moths (especially the winter moth) and sawflies are common pests of herbaceous plants, roses and a wide variety of shrubs. They mostly

feed on the foliage, disfiguring the plants by gnawing holes in the leaves or skeletonizing them and generally reducing plant vigour. Most caterpillars are readily controlled by general purpose contact insecticides including fenitrothion, gamma-HCH, permethrin, pirimiphos-methyl, pyrethrum, resmethrin and rotenone (derris). Various special formulations for roses and flowers are available and combined insecticide/fungicide products are marketed specifically for roses. Alternatively, it may be possible to use a preparation of *Bacillus thuringiensis* as a biological control measure.

Some caterpillars are more difficult to deal with. Gregarious types of web-spinning caterpillar may congregate on certain shrubs where they are protected by their webs. With these the best approach is to prune out and destroy the infested shoot tips. On various herbaceous plants, such as antirrhinum, chrysanthemum, dahlia, foxglove, hollyhock, iris, lupin, marigold and sunflower, caterpillars may tunnel into the stem, causing the plant to wilt and die. Insecticide sprays are ineffective against these and all that can be done is to remove the damaged stems and destroy the larvae inside.

Earwigs
These pests can cause serious damage to clematis, chrysanthemums, dahlias and other plants by chewing the petals, leaving them ragged and unsightly. With some plants a measure of control can be obtained by trapping, using upturned plant pots, loosely filled with straw, placed on top of the supporting canes. Another possibility is to apply an insecticide, such as gamma-HCH, permethrin or pirimiphos-methyl at dusk, after first shaking the blooms to dislodge any insects concealed inside.

Flea beetles
These tiny beetles chew small circular holes in the leaves of nasturtium, alyssum, anemones, wallflowers and stocks. They can be controlled by applying an insecticidal dust, such as gamma-HCH, pirimiphos-methyl or rotenone (derris) to the plants and the surrounding soil.

Frog-hoppers (cuckoo spit)
Little damage is done by the adult insects but the nymphs are sap suckers and can cause distortion of young growth. Infested plants can be spotted easily because of the spittle-like foam in which the nymphs are concealed. A wide range of plants can be affected, including euonymus, hebes, lavender, roses and many herbaceous plants. Light infestations may be controlled by picking off the nymphs but heavier attacks are more easily dealt with by the use of a forceful spray of a general purpose insecticide, such as dimethoate or permethrin.

Leafhoppers
Different species are found on a variety of garden and greenhouse plants. Three are of special importance:

    Glasshouse leafhopper is 2–3 mm long and pale yellow, with grey markings. It causes a coarse, pale mottling on the upper leaf surfaces of

tomato, fuchsia, pelargonium, primula and many other plants. Spray when damage is first seen with gamma-HCH, permethrin or pirimiphos-methyl. These chemicals are also available in smoke formulations for greenhouse fumigation.

Rhododendron leafhopper is a vividly coloured reddish-orange and turquoise green insect feeding on the foliage and flowers. It causes little direct damage but is responsible for infecting the flower buds with the fungus which causes bud blast. It can be controlled by spraying two or three times with dimethoate, gamma-HCH, permethrin or pirimiphos-methyl during August and September.

Rose leafhopper is a yellow insect which feeds on the undersides of the leaves, producing a whitish mottling on the upper surface. It is most damaging in dry weather, when it can cause premature leaf fall, but can be controlled readily by spraying with the above-mentioned insecticides as soon as damage is seen.

Lily beetle

These are small red beetles the larvae of which feed on the leaves, stems and seed pods of fritillaries, lilies and, occasionally, on Solomon's seal. The plump larvae are orange in colour but are frequently covered with black, slimy faeces. They are voracious feeders and can quickly strip the leaves from the plants. Small numbers of larvae may be picked off and destroyed, but it is more effective to spray the infested plants with an insecticide, such as fenitrothion, permethrin or pirimiphos-methyl. Be prepared to apply repeat treatments as it becomes necessary.

Narcissus fly

This is a major pest of cultivated narcissi and can also attack other bulbs, such as hippeastrum. The larvae tunnel into the centre of the bulb which then develops wet rot. Infested bulbs never flower but may produce thin, grass-like leaves. Prevent attack by dusting around the bulbs with gamma-HCH or pirimiphos-methyl, starting at the end of April and continuing at fortnightly intervals until July.

Rose leaf-rolling sawfly

A pest which is easily recognised by the appearance of leaflets rolled up into tight tubes containing the eggs and, later, the larvae. The pest is difficult to control but it is worth picking off and destroying the affected leaves. Treatment with an insecticide such as pirimiphos-methyl gives some protection.

Whitefly

Glasshouse whitefly can occur on many outdoor plants but is mainly a problem of plants grown under protection. Other species may also be of importance on certain ornamental shrubs.

Azalea and rhododendron whitefly – This species lays eggs on the

underside of the leaves in June and July and the yellowish-green 'scales' which hatch out stay on the underside of the leaves and suck sap from the plant. They do not develop further until the following May so that there is only one generation per year and the population builds up rather slowly. Heavy infestations can cause objectionable soiling of the leaves with honeydew and sooty mould. They can be controlled by repeat applications of dimethoate, permethrin, pirimiphos-methyl or pyrethrum in June and July.

Viburnum whitefly – The tiny, white, moth-like adults are present only during the summer on *Viburnum tinus*. The scale-like nymphs and pupae feed on the underside of the leaves, producing honeydew which encourages the growth of sooty mould. Heavy infestations can cause browning of the foliage and shoot die-back. The control measures are the same as for azalea and rhododendron whitefly.

Pest control – fruit

Aphids (greenfly, blackfly, etc.)
Sap-sucking insects which can be important on all types of fruit. They feed on soft, new growth and not only cause distortion and reduced vigour but are also important in the transmission of virus diseases. There are many different species. Some live on one type of host plant throughout the year. Most species, however, alternate between two hosts, one usually a woody plant on which they overwinter and feed while the new growth is soft in the spring, the other a herbaceous plant on which they feed in summer. Important species include the apple-grass aphid and woolly aphid on apples, leaf-curling plum aphid and mealy plum aphid on plums and damsons, the gooseberry aphid and redcurrant aphid on currants and gooseberries. The strawberry aphid is the main vector of virus diseases on this crop.

Aphids can be readily killed by spraying with systemic insecticides, such as dimethoate or heptenophos, or with contact-acting sprays, such as fenitrothion, malathion, pirimicarb, pirimiphos-methyl or rotenone (derris) in spring or early summer. Pirimicarb is of special interest as it does not affect beneficial insects such as ladybirds, lacewings or bees. A tar-oil winter wash applied when the trees or bushes are fully dormant can help to prevent trouble by killing the overwintering eggs. However, additional treatment with one of the above chemicals will often be needed during the growing season.

Big bud gall mite
This pest infests the buds of blackcurrant, causing them to become swollen and rounded. Infested buds fail to develop normally with a consequent reduction in cropping. The mites also transmit reversion disease which greatly weakens the bushes. It is difficult to eradicate gall mites once established but carbendazim fungicide gives some degree of protection in

addition to controlling fungal diseases. The spray should be applied as the first flowers open and on two further occasions at two-week intervals. As a preventative measure remove and burn any infested buds in early spring.

Blackcurrant leaf midge

Larvae of the midge attack the shoot tips, causing the young leaves to remain folded and twisted and the shoot growth to be stunted. The tips of the shoots should be sprayed with a contact insecticide, such as permethrin, as soon as the trouble is spotted but do not spray when the bushes are in flower.

Capsid bugs

These are sucking insects which feed on the leaves in spring, producing small holes which later enlarge to give the leaves a tattered appearance. The common green capsid feeds on a wide range of plants including apples, pears and blackcurrants. Like aphids, capsids are susceptible to many insecticides, including systemic chemicals, such as dimethoate, and contact chemicals, including fenitrothion, gamma-HCH, malathion, permethrin, pirimiphos-methyl, pyrethrum and rotenone (derris). Sprays should be applied soon after petal-fall.

Caterpillars

The caterpillars of several types of winter moth and tortrix moths attack the developing leaves, flowers and fruit of all types of fruit trees (especially apples) in spring. They can be controlled by various contact acting insecticides, such as fenitrothion, pirimiphos-methyl, permethrin, pyrethrum and rotenone (derris), applied when the green flower buds appear (apples), at petal-fall (pears), or at the white bud stage (plums). Grease bands applied round the trunks in November also reduce the problem by preventing the wingless female moths from reaching the branches where they lay their eggs. Bacterial products based on *Bacillus thuringiensis* provide another non-chemical method of dealing with caterpillar problems.

Codling moth caterpillars emerge and start feeding on apples in mid-summer, tunnelling into the core of the developing fruits and leaving them in July and August to overwinter. Control can be achieved by spraying with fenitrothion, permethrin or pirimiphos-methyl in mid-June and again in early July.

Raspberry beetle

The grubs of this small beetle feed on the developing fruits of raspberry and other cane fruit. They can be controlled by spraying with fenitrothion, malathion, permethrin or rotenone (derris). With raspberries spray at the first pink fruit stage; loganberries when about 80% of the blossom is over, repeating the treatment about two weeks later; blackberries just before the first flower opens.

Red spider mites

These tiny pests, only just visible to the naked eye, feed on the underside of the leaves causing them to discolour and dry up. They are a serious pest in greenhouses but also affect many outdoor plants, especially in hot summers. Apples, plums, raspberries, blackcurrants and strawberries are the most likely to be affected. Control can be achieved with various chemicals, including dimethoate, malathion and pirimiphos-methyl, and repeated treatments may be necessary.

Sawflies

The larvae of sawflies are similar to the caterpillars of moths and butterflies and cause similar damage. The species which attack currants and gooseberries are large and green, often with characteristic black spots, and can skeletonize the foliage very rapidly. Other species attack plums and apples, boring into the fruit and causing early fruit fall. Sawfly larvae are readily controlled by the same range of contact insecticides as those used to kill other caterpillars. They should be applied at the first signs of attack but not during the flowering period. Fruitlet feeding sawflies are controlled by spraying within seven days of petal-fall.

Scale insects

Sucking insects which form a shell-like covering, encrusting the bark and sometimes the fruits of fruit trees, bushes and canes, especially in sheltered situations. A tar-oil winter wash can be used to obtain control during the dormant season. During the growing season products based on malathion or pirimiphos-methyl can also be used in early July, repeated if necessary fourteen days later.

Strawberry beetle

These black beetles feed on the ripening fruit, removing seeds and damaging the flesh. Clearing the surface of the beds in autumn helps to reduce the numbers of this pest. Another preventative measure is to sink jam jars in the soil in spring to act as beetle traps. Scattering slug pellets based on methiocarb around the plants is also helpful.

Woolly aphids

Occurring commonly on apples and feeding through the bark of the branches, these have a cotton wool-like covering of wax. They cause the development of soft, warty growths which can provide entry points for canker disease. Control can be obtained by applying a systemic chemical, such as dimethoate or heptenophos, or a forceful spray of a contact insecticide, such as fenitrothion, malathion, pirimicarb or pirimiphos-methyl.

Pest control – vegetables

Cabbage caterpillars

Several species attack brassicas, the most common being the large and the small cabbage white butterflies and the cabbage moth. Eggs are laid, either singly or in batches, on the underside of the leaves and the caterpillars emerging from these eggs feed on the plant foliage for about a month before dropping off to pupate. Check brassicas regularly for the presence of eggs or young caterpillars and destroy any that are found. For bad infestations it may be easier to spray the crop with a general purpose insecticide. Products based on pyrethrum or pyrethroids, such as permethrin or resmethrin, are to be preferred because of their combination of low mammalian toxicity and high efficiency against caterpillars. An alternative to chemicals is biological control based on *Bacillus thuringiensis*, a bacterial agent specific against caterpillars.

Flea beetles

These are small, hopping beetles which feed on seedling brassicas and other plants of the brassica family, producing small, circular holes in the leaves. The larvae can also be damaging because they feed on plant roots. Protect susceptible seedlings by applying an insecticidal dust based on gamma-HCH, pirimiphos-methyl or rotenone (derris) to the seedlings and surrounding soil.

Lettuce root aphid

Colonies of yellowish, wingless aphids tend to develop on the roots of lettuce during the summer, causing the plants to wilt and possibly die in hot, dry weather. Some lettuce varieties, such as Avoncrisp and Avondefiance, are resistant to these pests but most common varieties are highly susceptible. Good hygiene, thorough cultivation and crop rotation help to reduce the risk of attack. Infested plants can be treated with heavy soil drenches of spray-strength solutions of malathion or pirimiphos-methyl.

Pea moth

Eggs are laid on the pea foliage and the caterpillars which emerge eat into the pods and feed on the developing peas for about a month before dropping to the soil, where they overwinter in cocoons. Egg laying is mostly restricted to the June/July period and the trouble can be avoided by adjusting the sowing date so as to avoid the crop coming into flower during this period. Alternatively, a general purpose insecticide, such as permethrin, pirimiphos-methyl, pyrethrum or resmethrin, can be applied about a week after the first flowering and a repeat application given about a fortnight later.

Root flies

The small, white grubs of these flies can be very damaging to the roots of several vegetable crops.

Cabbage fly attacks both leafy and root brassicas, turnips and swedes, killing young seedlings and reducing the cropping of established plants.

Carrot fly not only attacks carrots but also the roots of parsnips, celery and parsley. On carrots the first sign of attack is a reddening of the foliage, followed by stunting of growth. Initially they feed on the fine roots but later bore into the main taproot, making it unusable. Adults of the first generation emerge in May to June and the second generation in August to September. Consequently some measure of control can be obtained by delaying sowing until late May or early June, and then lifting the crop early before the second generation of flies are active.

Onion fly feeds on the bulbs and stem bases of onions and also attacks shallots and leeks. Young plants wilt and may die and the tissues of older plants become soft and rotten.

Early attacks by root fly pests can be controlled by applying soil insecticides, such as bromophos, gamma-HCH (not on onion), phoxim or pirimiphos-methyl, to the seed drills and around transplanted seedlings. Use heavy soil drenches of spray-strength pirimiphos-methyl around the plants to check infestations on established plants.

Whitefly

Both the adults and developing larvae of these tiny, white, moth-like insects are sap-feeders which infest the underside of the leaves of brassicas. Like other sap-feeders they excrete sticky honeydew which quickly becomes covered with sooty mould. Whitefly are difficult to control because some of the immature stages are highly resistant to most insecticides. Repeat sprays of pyrethrum or pyrethroid chemicals, such as permethrin, applied at fortnightly intervals give some control. Dimethoate, malathion and pirimiphos-methyl can also be used. At the end of the season any infested plants should be pulled up and burnt to prevent carry over of the pest.

Disease control – general

Grey mould *(Botrytis cinerea)*

Grey mould is a very common and widespread disease affecting the flowers, buds, leaves, stems and fruit of many host plants. It first shows up as a browning of the infected tissues. Later, especially in humid conditions, the diseased parts become covered with a grey growth of mould. In the control of this disease the first essential is to practice good plant hygiene, removing and destroying any infected tissues. Good ventilation should be aimed at in the greenhouse while, out of doors, care must be taken to avoid overcrowding, especially in damp, shady situations. Plants can be protected from attack by applying routine sprays of benomyl, carbendazim or thiophanate-methyl but too regular use may lead to a build-up of resistant strains of the fungus. Under glass, tecnazene smokes should be used.

Honey fungus *(Armillaria mellea)*

This is a very important disease since it can attack and kill almost all types of woody plant and some herbaceous species. The initial symptoms are usually an out-of-season yellowing and browning of the foliage, though sometimes the first sign of attack is that the tree or shrub fails to come into leaf in the spring. Honey fungus attack is usually associated with the presence of a fern-like, white fungal growth between the bark and the wood at the base of the trunk. Brownish-black fungal strands (bootlaces) are found in the soil around the infected plants. Another indication of the presence of the fungus is the development of clusters of yellow or tawny toadstools on or around the base of the affected tree or shrub. Dead trees or shrubs should be dug up, together with as much root as possible. Any fungal 'bootlaces' should also be removed. When replacing the soil, each layer should be drenched with tar-oil emulsion. This treatment should also be applied around nearby plants to prevent the spread of the disease. Wherever possible try to replace infected plants with trees and shrubs which are less susceptible to the disease.

Powdery mildew

This disease, which shows up as a whitish, powdery covering on stems, leaves, buds, flowers and fruit, attacks a wide variety of vegetables, decorative plants, fruit trees and bushes. Affected tissues usually become discoloured and distorted, while the growth of the plant is weakened. With apples and gooseberries some infected shoots are removed by winter pruning. Primary infected shoots on apple trees should also be pruned out in the spring. In all cases it is important to start a programme of repeat spray applications as soon as there are signs of attack using a systemic fungicide such as benomyl, carbendazim or thiophanate-methyl.

Rusts

Rust diseases affect many fruit trees, shrubs, vegetables and ornamental plants. They become evident as yellow, orange, brown or black pustules on the foliage and stems of infected plants. Where the pustules develop on the underside of the leaves, corresponding yellowish spots appear on the upper surface. Infected leaves wither and fall prematurely, thus severely weakening the plants. At the first signs of disease any infected leaves should be removed and destroyed and a fungicidal spray programme initiated, applying the sprays at two – three week intervals. Suitable fungicides include copper products, mancozeb, myclobutanil, propiconazole and triforine.

Disease control – ornamentals

Azalea gall

This is a common problem on evergreen azaleas, especially in the greenhouse. First symptoms of the disease are the appearance of round

galls on the leaves and flower buds. The galls are red at first but later turn a chalky-white when the spores develop. Control is mainly by picking off and destroying the galls, but some protection against further attack can be obtained by spraying with a copper fungicide.

Bulb and corm disease
At the end of the growing season it is desirable to lift and destroy any bulb or corm which has produced unhealthy foliage. Lift also all the related bulbs or corms and dip them in a solution of benomyl, carbendazim or thiophanate-methyl as a protective treatment.

Cankers
Cankers on ornamental malus can be caused by a variety of fungi and microbial organisms. They appear first as areas of damaged bark, under which the active cambial layer has been killed. When the entire branch is girdled with a canker all growth beyond this point ceases and the branch dies. In the early stages cankers can be treated by paring off the damaged tissues and covering the wound with a canker paint. Branches which have been completely girdled should be pruned off below the canker and canker paint used to seal the bare surface.

Chrysanthemum brown rust
A disease of outdoor chrysanthemums under moist conditions. It appears first on the lower leaves, on the undersides, as raised brown pustules. Mancozeb may be used as a protective treatment or control with propiconazole applied at the first signs of infection.

Chrysanthemum petal blight
Small brown spots develop on the tips of the outer florets and spread inwards. The florets turn brown and shrivel and the whole bloom eventually becomes affected. Control by repeat applications of mancozeb, starting when the first disease symptoms appear.

Chrysanthemum white rust
A more serious disease than the commoner brown rust. It differs in that the pustules which develop on the leaves are a pale pinkish-buff colour at first and gradually develop into a whitish coating before turning brown and necrotic. The disease survives on growing plants, the green parts of dormant stools and on chrysanthemum debris. Badly affected plants should be destroyed to prevent the disease from spreading and the rest should be treated with propiconazole as a protective spray or with a product containing triforine.

Clematis wilt
A destructive disease causing the sudden death of one or more shoots. Wilted shoots do not recover but the disease does not normally spread below soil level so that new, healthy shoots often grow from the base.

Treatment consists of cutting back to healthy tissue and painting the cut with a pruning wound product. As a preventative measure new shoots should be given two or three sprays with benomyl, carbendazim or a copper fungicide at fortnightly intervals.

Clubroot
Wallflowers and stocks can be attacked by this disease in the same way as brassica vegetables, the affected roots becoming swollen and distorted and the whole plant stunted. Control by applying calomel (mercurous chloride) or thiophanate-methyl to the seed drills and to the seedling roots when transplanting.

Fireblight
A disease which can have disastrous effects on certain trees and shrubs belonging to the rose family, such as chaenomeles, cotoneaster, hawthorn and pyracantha. The first signs are that the flowers and leaves turn brown and die, so that the affected branches look as though they had been scorched by fire. A glistening white slime may also exude under warm, moist conditions and the underlying wood turns reddish. The disease spreads rapidly and generally kills the shrub or tree. If the disease is detected before it has spread too far infected shoots should be cut out 60 cm (2 ft) below the obviously diseased parts and burnt. Pruning tools should be carefully disinfected after use to avoid spreading the disease.

Geranium black-leg
A disease which commonly causes trouble on geranium cuttings where a blackening begins at the base of the cutting and spreads upwards. It is controlled by good plant hygiene and by dipping the cutting in a rooting powder containing a fungicide before inserting it into the growing compost.

Leaf spot diseases
Many ornamentals can be attacked by leaf-spotting fungi which produce brown, often circular spots on the leaves of plants lacking in vigour. Remove and burn diseased leaves. Spray with a systemic fungicide or with mancozeb and improve the cultural conditions.

Paeony wilt
This disease attacks herbaceous and tree paeonies and causes browning, withering and, finally, death of the affected shoots. It can also cause browning and death of the flower buds. Affected tissues may become covered with grey, velvety fungal growth in wet weather. Treat by removing the affected shoots, cutting out well below the soil level in the case of herbaceous paeonies, and burning them. Dust the clumps with a copper dust and spray with a systemic fungicide, such as benomyl, carbendazim, propiconazole or thiophanate-methyl, soon after the leaves emerge, repeating at fortnightly intervals until flowering. Spray again after flowering if necessary.

Rhododendron bud-blast

Infected flower buds turn brown and dry out during the winter and fail to open in the spring. This disease gains entry through wounds made in the flower buds by rhododendron leaf hoppers, so these need to be controlled. Infected buds should be removed and destroyed.

Rose black spot

This widespread disease appears as circular dark spots on the leaves and young stems. Infected leaves later turn yellow and fall early. The fungus overwinters in fallen leaves and infected bud scales. Measures which help to prevent black spot include correct planting, good cultural treatment, collecting and burning fallen rose leaves in autumn and pruning and destroying any shoots showing black scabs in the spring. A fungicidal spray should be applied immediately after spring pruning and followed by a programme of sprays at 10–14 day intervals. Most garden fungicides with a systemic action control black spot and several effective fungicide/insecticide combinations are marketed specifically for use on roses.

Rose rust

A damaging disease commonest in the south and east but also extending into the midlands. It appears on the leaves in summer as orange pustules which become dark brown in autumn. Spores overwinter on fallen leaves and other plant debris. Cultural measures which help to prevent infection are the same as for black spot. Propiconazole is recommended for control of rose rust and a new fungicide, myclobutanil, has recently appeared on the market for control of this and other rose diseases. Reasonable control can also be expected using products containing triforine.

Silver leaf

The disease affects a number of ornamental trees and shrubs, including cotoneaster, eucalyptus, laburnum, poplars and sorbus, as well as prunus. For control measures see entry under diseases in fruit.

Tulip fire

This disease is spread by infected bulbs which produce distorted shoots and leaves. The malformed shoots wither and become covered with grey mould in moist conditions. Black resting bodies of the fungus are produced by diseased plants and can remain viable in the soil for up to two years. Bulbs producing infected shoots must be lifted and destroyed promptly. At the end of the season any diseased bulbs should be destroyed and healthy bulbs protected by a dip treatment with benomyl or carbendazim. Growing plants can be protected by spraying with benomyl, carbendazim, mancozeb or thiophanate-methyl.

Disease control – fruit

American gooseberry mildew

This is a disease common both on blackcurrants and gooseberries. It appears as a white powdery covering of the young leaves, shoots and buds in early summer. Later the disease infects the developing fruits which become discoloured. At the first signs of disease the bushes should be sprayed with benomyl, bupirimate + triforine, carbendazim, a suitable form of copper or thiophanate-methyl and the treatment should be repeated at fortnightly intervals. Sulphur sprays also provide a degree of protection but must not be used on sulphur-shy varieties. In early autumn any infected shoot tips should be pruned off and the prunings destroyed.

Bacterial canker

Worst on cherries and plums but all types of stone fruit and ornamental prunus can be affected. The disease shows first as elongated depressions in the bark which exude gum. The leaves become stunted and yellow and affected branches may die back completely. Dark brown circular spots may also develop on the leaves and these may link together before the centres drop out, producing a 'shot-hole' effect. Spray cherries with Bordeaux mixture or another copper fungicide in mid-August, mid-September and mid-October or, if autumn spraying is omitted, spray just before the blossom opens and again at petal fall. To protect young, non-fruiting plums and ornamental prunus spray three weeks after petal fall and repeat a fortnight later. Infected branches should be cut out and burnt.

Cane blight

The disease attacks raspberries and is caused by a fungus which enters the plant at the base of the canes. Infected canes show a dark area at ground level and become very brittle. The leaves on infected canes wither. Remove and burn all infected canes by cutting well below soil level and spray new growth regularly with Bordeaux mixture or another copper fungicide.

Cane spot

Raspberries, loganberries and hybrid berries are all liable to attack by this disease. Small purple spots develop on the canes in early summer. The spots then elongate and turn whitish, with a purple border, later splitting and forming cankers. Spray with benomyl, carbendazim, copper or thiophanate-methyl at fortnightly intervals until the start of flowering.

Canker

Apples, pears and some ornamental trees can be affected. The disease first appears as sunken areas in the bark. Later the bark in the central area of the canker dies and crumbles away. Where the canker encircles the stem the whole branch dies. Treat by paring away the diseased tissue and painting the exposed surface with a canker paint (pruning wound product).

Fungicidal sprays applied against scab and mildew also help to reduce the canker problem.

Coral spot
Redcurrants are liable to attack by this disease which causes whole branches to die back. It is recognised by the appearance of pinhead-size, red pustules on the dying branches. Treat by pruning out dead shoots and painting the cut surfaces with a pruning wound product.

Currant leaf spot
This is a common disease of all types of currant and gooseberries. Small, irregular brown blotches develop on the leaves from May onwards and the infected leaves fall early, thus reducing the vigour of the bushes. Collect and destroy infected leaves and treat the bushes with a protective spray of mancozeb after flowering. Benomyl, bupirimate + triforine, carbendazim or thiophanate-methyl can also be used at the young flowering stage and copper can be applied after harvest.

Gooseberry cluster cup
A rust disease which occurs mostly in Scotland. The orange and red pustules appear on the lower leaves and fruits in early summer, later developing into small cluster cups. The spores produced infect sedges, which are alternate hosts to the fungus during winter and provide a source of reinfection in the following year. Spraying with a copper fungicide or mancozeb may control this disease, provided that the first application is made about a fortnight before flowering.

Grey mould
A common problem in strawberries which causes a brownish-grey rot of the fruit following early infection of the flowers. Control by spraying with a product containing benomyl, carbendazim or thiophanate-methyl at the early blossom stage (before the disease appears) and, if necessary, give repeat treatments at 10–14 day intervals.

Peach leaf curl
Peaches, nectarines, flowering almonds and other related prunus are liable to be attacked. Shortly after bud-burst some developing leaves become swollen and distorted, forming yellowish or reddish blisters. Later the leaves become covered with a whitish bloom, turn black and fall prematurely. Control by spraying with a copper fungicide after leaf-fall in the autumn and, again, in late January, repeating in early February. The removal and destruction of infected leaves in early summer also helps to reduce the spread of the disease.

Plum rust
Bright yellow spotting occurs on the upper leaf surface of trees affected with the disease and orange or brown spores are produced from the lower

surface. Infected leaves turn yellow and fall early. Collecting and destroying infected leaves reduces the carry-over of the disease to the next year. It is not usually worth spraying against this disease but a measure of protection can be obtained by spraying with a copper fungicide or mancozeb at the first signs of the disease.

Powdery mildew

This disease is commonest on apples. It first shows up in spring, when the emerging shoots and flower trusses appear silvery grey due to the covering of fungal spores. Diseased shoots are stunted and infected flowers do not set fruit. The primary infection is the source of more general infection during summer, so that it is important to remove and destroy these silvered shoots and flower trusses at an early stage. This treatment may be followed by application of a series of sprays at two-week intervals , starting at bud-burst, using such fungicides as benomyl, bupirimate + triforine, carbendazim or thiophanate-methyl.

A different species of mildew affects peaches and is commonest under glass, appearing as a whitish powder on the leaves, buds and shoots. Control by cutting off any heavily mildewed shoots and then spray at fortnightly intervals with one of the fungicides mentioned above or with copper or sulphur.

Scab

A common disease on apples and pears. Infected leaves develop olive-green powdery blotches and blackish scabs form on the fruits. In areas where the disease is a problem reasonable protection can be obtained by applying a programme of four sprays at intervals of two – three weeks, starting when green flower buds first appear. A wide range of fungicides are suitable, including benomyl, bupirimate + triforine, carbendazim, copper, sulphur (not on pears or sulphur-shy varieties of apple) and thiophanate-methyl.

Silver leaf

A disease commonest on plums but also capable of infecting various other fruit and ornamental trees. The first sign is a silvering of the foliage. Later there is progressive die-back of infected branches and small, bracket-shaped fungal fruiting bodies may grow on the dead wood. Cross sections of infected branches show a purple staining of the wood. Control by cutting back affected branches to about 15 cm (6 in) below the level of the stained wood and paint the cut surface with a pruning wound product or a *Trichoderma* preparation.

Spur blight

This is a serious disease of raspberries and can also infect loganberries. Infection occurs in early summer but the first signs of attack are in early August when purple lesions develop around the nodes of the canes. These turn silver and become dotted with tiny black spots, where the spores are

produced which infect new canes in spring. Cut out and destroy infected canes and control by spraying with a fungicide three or four times at fortnightly intervals, starting when the new canes have emerged. Suitable chemicals include benomyl, carbendazim, copper formulations and thiophanate-methyl.

Strawberry mildew

Commonest on protected crops this disease is seen in spring as dark patches on the upper leaf surface, with whitish-grey spores on the underside. Affected leaves curl upwards and the flowers and berries shrivel. The variety *Cambridge Favourite* is particularly susceptible. Dust with sulphur, commencing pre-blossom in early spring and repeating at 10–14 day intervals, or apply a systemic fungicide.

Disease control – vegetables

Chocolate spot

This is a disease of over-wintered broad beans and first appears in the form of reddish-purple spots on the leaves, stems and pods. The spots later merge together and the affected tissues turn black and rot. The disease is favoured by damp conditions, shade and overcrowding. Fortnightly spraying with benomyl, carbendazim or copper until flowering help to reduce the spread of the disease.

Club root

A serious disease of brassicas, swedes and turnips. The roots of infected plants become thickened and distorted, the lateral roots developing elongated galls (finger and toe symptoms). As a result of the root damage the top growth of infected plants becomes stunted and may turn a reddish-purple colour. The disease is favoured by poor drainage and acid conditions so that heavy soils need to be improved by working in plenty of organic matter and acid soils benefit from the application of lime. Some measure of control can be obtained by applying mercurous chloride (calomel) or thiophanate-methyl, either to the seedling roots at planting out or into the planting hole.

Downy mildew

Various vegetables can be affected, the first signs of the disease being yellowish patches on the upper leaf surface corresponding to areas of white or purplish mould growth below. Mildew can be troublesome on beet, brassicas, lettuce, onions, peas, radishes, spinach, swedes and turnips and its spread can be controlled by repeat sprays of mancozeb, thiram or copper.

Onion white rot
A very common disease of onions and leeks which may also affect chives, garlic and shallots. Infected leaves turn yellow and begin to die back; later a white, fluffy mould growth develops on the bulbs. The disease is soil-borne and, once established, it cannot be eradicated. Infected plant material should on no account be composted as this is a sure way of spreading the trouble. However, a fair measure of control may be obtained by spraying with benomyl during the growing season.

Potato and tomato blight
Dark, brownish-black blotches develop on the leaves, particularly towards the tips and along the leaf margins. In moist conditions these blotches rapidly enlarge and a white mould grows on the underside of the leaves. In such conditions the whole top growth may then rot and collapse. Disease spores washed down into the soil infect the tubers which also become discoloured and rot. Tomato fruits also become infected and rapidly rot before picking or on storage. At the first sign of infection a programme of regular spraying at ten day intervals should be started, using either a copper fungicide or a product containing mancozeb.

Weed control
With dense plantings of bedding plants no chemical weedkillers can be used and only hand-weeding or the use of a small onion hoe is possible. In open plantings of roses, shrubs, herbaceous perennials, fruit trees and bushes and some vegetables, however, it is possible to control broad-leaved weeds and grasses by applying certain non-persistent weedkillers selectively to the weed growth while avoiding contact with the garden plants. Where there is a general infestation of weeds the treatment is best applied using a short sprinkler bar fitted in place of the rose on a watering can or a special applicator. For control of light, localized weed patches some products are formulated specially for application as spot treatments.

The following chemicals are suitable for selective application:

Diquat + paraquat
This ready-mixed product gives a quick kill of the top growth of weeds, both broad-leaved types and grasses, but many perennial weeds develop regrowth so that the treatment must be repeated. The chemical is highly rain-fast so that, even if rain falls immediately after application, its action is not affected. The chemical is inactivated on contact with the soil and has no residual effect. However, in the absence of soil disturbance, further germination of weed seeds is not stimulated as it is by hoeing. The mixture has a rapid scorching effect on leaves and green stems but is not absorbed through mature, brown bark. It may thus be safely applied right up to the base of roses and other woody plants and, in the winter, may be used to clean up the weeds in raspberry rows. Weed kill at this time of year may

take several weeks but the final effect is excellent. The mixture may also be used to kill the young green suckers of rose, lilac, etc., the root suckers of apples, pears and stone fruit as well as unwanted young raspberry canes and strawberry runners.

If using this product among vegetables special care must be taken near onions, shallots and leeks as even slight contact with the crop foliage can lead to rotting at the base of the plant.

Glyphosate

This chemical also is non-residual, it is inactivated in the soil where it is then biodegraded. It is, however, highly systemic, moving readily from the leaves into the plant root system and is thus effective against many perennial weeds as well as annuals. It is absorbed into plant tissues rather slowly so that a rain-free period of at least six hours after application is needed for treatment to be fully effective. It may take some weeks to achieve a complete kill, especially on perennial weeds. Because glyphosate moves so freely within the plant great care needs to be taken to avoid all contact with cultivated plants. For treating scattered weeds it is easier to do this using the gel formulation, painted onto individual weeds, than by application of the liquid formulation.

Dalapon

A systemic grass-killing chemical with more limited uses than the above. It is not inactivated on contact with the soil but persists for several weeks before being leached out by rainfall. It can be used in the autumn or early spring when the crop plants are dormant to control couch and other grass weeds around the base of apple and pear trees, currants, gooseberries and raspberries. The plants must have been established for at least three – four years and the spray must be directed so as to avoid them. The treatment should not be used around plums or other stone fruit. Broad-leaved weeds are not controlled.

In the vegetable garden dalapon can be used on asparagus in spring, before the spears emerge, or as a spot treatment in summer after cutting, avoiding the fern. Well established rhubarb can also be treated in spring or autumn but the crowns and leaves should be protected to minimize contact with the spray.

Certain weedkillers have a truly selective mode of action (i.e. – they kill the weeds without affecting the crop plants) so that in some situations they can be applied as overall treatments to whole beds.

These chemicals are:

Alloxydim-sodium

A selective, post-emergence weedkiller effective against most grass weeds but, unfortunately, not annual meadow grass. It can be applied as an overall spray without affecting broad-leaved ornamental plants or broad-leaved weeds but should not be used on any food crops. The chemical is most

effective when grass weeds are growing actively and its action needs at least two hours dry weather after application.

Dichlobenil
A residual chemical acting through the soil which controls annual and many perennial weeds, including grass weeds. It can be used in rose beds and among some ornamental trees and shrubs established for at least two years, but must not be used where herbaceous ornamentals are present. It can also be applied around apples, pears, bush and cane fruit, again provided that the plantings have been established for at least two years. The best results are obtained by applying the granules evenly in early spring to moist soil, ideally just before rain. The effects of the treatment persist for several months.

Propachlor
A residual, soil-acting weedkiller which controls germinating annual weeds but not weeds which are already established. It is best applied immediately after sowing or planting and keeps the ground clean for up to six – eight weeks. It may be used on a range of vegetables, including beans, brassicas, kale, leeks, onions and swedes, as well as on strawberries, roses, ornamental shrubs, herbaceous perennials and a number of bedding plants.

Simazine
Another residual, soil-acting weedkiller but more persistent than propachlor. It can be used to control germinating annual broad-leaved and grass weeds in a wide range of established woody ornamentals and fruit. Some commonly grown ornamentals, however, are susceptible to simazine and should not be included in shrub borders where it is planned to use this chemical. It should be applied to ground clear of emerged weeds as the chemical has little or no effect on weeds which are already established. If the soil is not disturbed, however, it prevents the establishment of weed seedlings for the whole season. The best results are obtained by application to a firm, moist soil surface in early spring. The treatment can be safely applied on established roses and shrubs but not on newly planted bushes or on light sandy soil. It should not be used if any herbaceous plants are present.

Simazine can be used to maintain weed-free conditions around top, bush and cane fruit (with the exception of plums and other stone fruit) provided that the plantings have been established for at least twelve months. Best results are obtained by application in February or March. It can also be applied from July to December over strawberry beds established for at least six months, but should not be used on the varieties *Huxley Giant, Madame Moutot* or *Regina*.

Among vegetable crops simazine is recommended for use in sweetcorn. It can also be used in asparagus and rhubarb established for at least twelve months. No crop should be sown for at least seven months after applying this chemical.

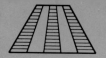

Lawn chemicals

Insect pests

The main insect pests of lawns are chafer grubs and leatherjackets, both of which are root feeders. Grasses attacked by these pests make poor growth and wilt readily under dry conditions. Secondary damage may be caused by birds tearing out the grass when searching for grubs. Leatherjackets, the grubs of crane flies or daddy-longlegs, are greyish brown in colour and have a tough, wrinkled skin. They are legless and have no distinct head. Chafer grubs, on the other hand are whitish, fleshy creatures with a large brown head and three pairs of legs. Their bodies are characteristically curved round like a letter 'C'. Both types of pests are most active in moist weather in spring, early summer and autumn, when they move into the upper layers of the soil.

Control can be achieved by applying a drenching spray of carbaryl or pirimiphos-methyl in spring or early autumn. Carbaryl is also available mixed with a high phosphate fertiliser. Applied in the autumn this product encourages root growth through the winter and helps to offset any root damage caused by the pests.

Ants may sometimes cause trouble on lawns where the hills they produce are disfiguring and can cause difficulty with mowing. They are readily controlled by the soil insecticides mentioned above or by a variety of antkillers based on such chemicals as gamma-HCH, phoxim or pirimicarb. In many cases it will be necessary to level the ant-hills before mowing.

Worms

Earthworms have both beneficial and harmful effects on lawns. On the credit side, their tunnelling through the soil helps aeration. On the other hand, worm casts on the surface are a nuisance as, when flattened by a mower or the feet, they impede drainage and form bare patches where coarse grasses and other weeds may become established. It must be stressed that only one or two of the 20 or so species of earthworm found in gardens actually produce casts on the surface. Worms are favoured by moist, loamy soil containing decomposing organic matter. They are less common in sandy soils and not often found under acid soil conditions. Consequently their numbers tend to build up if lawn clippings are left on the surface, while the use of acid fertilisers, such as sulphate of ammonia, has the opposite effect.

Worm activity is greatest in late spring and early autumn and these are the best times for applying control treatments. Carbaryl can be used as

a heavy drenching spray or in the form of granules combined with fertiliser. Boots Total Lawn Treatment, which contains benazolin with other weed-killers together with the mosskiller dichlorophen, is also recommended for control of worms.

Diseases

Turf grasses can be attacked by a number of disease-causing fungi, the commonest of which are the following:

Fusarium patch

The first symptoms of this disease are the appearance of small patches of yellowish, dying grass, the conditions most conducive to the disease being warm, humid weather in autumn or sometimes in spring. Once the infection has become established the affected patches may join together so that relatively large areas of grass become damaged. The disease is favoured by lush grass growth so that high-nitrogen fertilisers should not be applied in late summer or autumn.

Red thread

A disease commonest around mid-summer. Affected grass takes on a bleached appearance and, in humid weather, small, pink needles of fungus develop on the blades and leaf sheaths of the grass. The disease does not kill the grass and the only treatment needed may be to apply a high nitrogen fertiliser.

Dollar spot

First appears as small, circular bleached spots up to 3–5 cm (1–2 in) in diameter. As the disease develops the individual spots may join up to form larger patches.

All three of these diseases can be controlled by repeated spray applications of benomyl, carbendazim, dichlorophen or thiophanate-methyl. Combinations of dichlorophen with mosskillers or fertiliser may also be used.

Toadstools

Although not parasitic on the grasses, these fungi can damage and disfigure lawns. The infestations commonly start at a central point and then spread out in ever-widening circles, producing rings of toadstools, mushrooms or puff-balls.

The most disfiguring type of fairy ring is caused by *Marasmius oreades* which produces a band of stunted or dead grass sandwiched between two green zones where the grass has been stimulated. Small brown toadstools then develop in the middle zone.

Some control of toadstools can be obtained by applying dichlorophen as a spray or in granular form combined with a fertiliser.

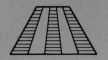

Broad-leaved weeds

Most modern selective weedkillers, such as 2, 4–D, dicamba, MCPA and mecoprop (sometimes called hormone weedkillers because they act in a similar manner to naturally occurring plant hormones) work by disrupting the growth of broad-leaved weeds while not affecting established grasses. They are all related chemically but each has its own particular spectrum of activity. Thus lawn weedkiller products are generally based on mixtures of two or more of the above chemicals. One product also contains benazolin which is particularly effective on weeds belonging the the chickweed family.

Although the chemicals have no effect on established grass they can cause damage to seedling grasses and newly laid turf so that they must not be used on new lawns during the first six months of establishment. Furthermore, it takes some time for residues in the treated foliage to break down and, for this reason, clippings from the first three or four mowings must not be used as surface mulches around growing plants. Instead, the clippings should be composted for at least three months or else discarded. The chemicals may also persist in the soil for some weeks after application, particularly under dry conditions. Consequently it is recommended that the reseeding of any bare patches should be delayed for about six weeks following the use of a selective lawn weedkiller.

Since these chemicals act by disorganising the growth processes of the weeds they perform best when the weed plants are in active growth. This limits their use broadly to the period between mid-April and mid-September and, even during this time, they should not be used in drought conditions unless the lawn is being irrigated regularly. Ideal conditions for treatment are when the soil is moist but the weed foliage is dry. In order to ensure that the weeds have sufficient leaf area to absorb the chemical, and to allow time for it to be translocated within the plants, do not mow for three or four days before or after treatment.

A regular programme of mowing combined with fertiliser application goes a long way towards minimizing lawn weed problems. The fertiliser strengthens the grass so that it competes more strongly against the weeds. Sulphate of ammonia in particular not only boosts the grass growth but also helps to produce acid conditions which favour the finer grasses while discouraging the growth of many weeds. Lawn fertiliser can be applied either prior to application of the weedkiller or as a combined 'feed and weed' treatment.

The initial effect of selective lawn weedkillers is to stimulate the broad-leaved weeds into wild and deformed growth, with the result that at first they appear to benefit from the treatment. It can take several weeks before the weeds are finally killed. The susceptibility of lawn weeds to these products varies widely and, although many will usually succumb to a single treatment, others may require a repeat treatment five or six weeks later. Species which are normally fairly easy to control include daisy (Bellis perennis), mouse-ear chickweed (Cerastium holosteoides), smooth

hawk's-beard *(Crepis capillaris)*, mouse-ear hawkweed *(Hieracium pilosella)*, cat's-ear *(Hypochaeris radicata)*, plantains *(Plantago* spp), creeping buttercup *(Ranunculus repens)*, pearlwort *(Sagina procumbens)*, common chickweed *(Stellaria media)*, dandelion *(Taraxacum officinale)* and white clover *(Trifolium repens)*.

The following are some of the more resistant lawn weeds: yarrow *(Achillea millefolium)*, dove's-foot cranesbill *(Geranium molle)*, bird's-foot trefoil *(Lotus corniculatus)*, lesser celandine *(Ranunculus ficaria)* and lesser trefoil *(Trifolium dubium)*. These species are best controlled by using the higher recommended rates of weedkiller but, even then, more than one repeat treatment may be needed. The blue flowered speedwells *(Veronica* spp.*)* and the tiny moss-like mind-your-own-business *(Soleilrolia soleirolii)* are particularly difficult to eradicate as they are resistant to lawn weedkillers. They can be checked to some extent by spraying with dilute tar oil formulations. These, however, are not truly selective and can cause serious damage to the lawn grasses. Field woodrush *(Luzula campestris)* is also resistant to lawn weedkillers. Applying ground chalk or limestone in winter, however, is a useful deterrent.

Most garden plants are susceptible to the effects of very small traces of selective lawn weedkillers. Great care must be taken to avoid drift of spray or any other accidental contact with garden plants when treating lawns, especially near greenhouses. Care is also necessary to avoid contaminating equipment. A separate sprayer or watering can should be employed for the application of lawn weedkillers and any vessels used in mixing up spray solutions must be carefully washed after use.

Weedkiller formulations

Lawn weedkillers intended for overall application are available as:
● Liquids or soluble powders for application in solution. Fertiliser or mosskiller may also be included.
● Granular feed and weed products for direct application. Mosskiller may also be included and one product is additionally recommended for use against earthworms.

Various products are also formulated specifically for use on small areas or as spot treatments. These include:
● Ready-to-use (trigger grip) sprayers.
● Aerosol sprays.
● Wax sticks or sponge applicators for wiping onto individual weeds.
● Granule applicators for spot treatment.

Application of lawn chemicals

The first essential is to follow the directions given on the product label. Sometimes the directions are in the form of a booklet attached to the

container and this should be read carefully in order to obtain the best results from the treatment. Applying rates which are too low may be ineffective while excessively high rates can lead to grass damage. High rates may also be less effective in controlling the weeds as too great a scorching effect may reduce the systemic action of the chemical.

When applying liquid products the diluted solution should be distributed evenly over the specified area. In the case of small or medium size lawns this is best done with a watering can fitted with a fine rose or a sprinkler bar. For larger areas, however, the use of a pressurized sprayer is recommended as this will permit even coverage with a much smaller volume of liquid. Since each measure of concentrated product is designed to treat a specified area of lawn this means that higher concentrations are required when using a sprayer than when applying by watering can.

With products applied as granules or powder, even distribution at the recommended rate is again the key to success. The job can be done by hand but it is difficult to achieve even coverage by this method. The use of a specially designed lawn fertiliser spreader not only makes the task simpler but also ensures uniform coverage, provided that care is taken to avoid overlapping.

Spot treatments should be applied according to the manufacturers recommendations. The products are specially packaged to be suitable for treating small areas and may be ideal as follow-up treatments following an overall application. The non-selective, non-residual chemical glyphosate in its gel form may be used as a spot treatment on dandelions, docks and other flat weeds when painted onto the leaves of individual weeds, so long as care is taken to avoid contact with the lawn grasses.

Coarse grasses

Fine turf is always liable to invasion by clumps of coarse grasses, such as soft-grass (Holcus mollis) and Yorkshire fog (Dactylis glomerata). These need to be eliminated as soon as they are spotted. They are best lifted out carefully using a garden fork. Larger areas can then be re-seeded or re-turfed. Alternatively the patches of rogue grass can be killed by painting the leaves with a gel formulation of glyphosate.

Mosses

Invasion by mosses is a recurrent problem on many lawns, especially when grass growth is poor because of low fertility, waterlogging or shading. Such infestations tend to become more noticeable in winter because moss flourishes in conditions of low light and cold when the grass is not growing. Regular fertiliser application, coupled with improved drainage and good soil aeration, greatly reduces the degree of infestation. Raising the height of the mower is also beneficial but, even so, it is usually necessary to use chemical control methods if the aim is complete elimination of the moss.

The traditional method of moss control is the application of lawn sand, based on a mixture of ferrous sulphate, sulphate of ammonia and coarse sand. This treatment kills the moss and, at the same time, encourages strong grass growth. A drawback of the treatment is that the treated turf temporarily develops an unsightly blue-black colour. The discolouration is lessened by using one of the newer liquid or soluble powder preparations.

An additional mosskilling chemical which also has a contact effect on existing moss growth is dichlorophen, available by itself or in mixture with other mosskillers and/or fertiliser. Chloroxuron, by contrast, has a residual effect which can last for several months but has little contact action and, therefore, is formulated as a mixture with various other contact acting chemicals such as dichlorophen, ferrous sulphate or the different iron salt ferric sulphate.

Dilute solutions of some tar oil products are recommended for killing mosses on lawns, in addition to liverworts, lichens and algae. The effect is purely a contact scorching and the grass is scorched as well as the weeds, but only temporarily. The treatment is most likely to be of use where there are other highly resistant weeds, such as speedwell or mind-your-own-business, together with the moss.

Lichens and algae

Algal infestation shows up as blackened areas of lawn where the grass is covered by a gelatinous, blue-green mass of algae. This growth can be killed by the application of a dichlorophen-based product or a mosskiller containing ferrous sulphate. Lawns may also become infested with the lichen *Peltigera canina*, easily identified by its flat, leafy lobes which are brownish above and silvery below. The presence of this lichen in the lawn is an indication of low fertility so that application of fertiliser is recommended. A quick kill can be obtained by the use of dichlorophen or, at the expense of temporary grass scorching, a tar oil formulation.

Greenhouse chemicals

Disinfectants

Greenhouses provide an environment in which many pests and diseases are able to multiply rapidly during the growing season. The warm, moist conditions also encourage the growth of algae, moulds, mosses and lichens. A regular programme of greenhouse sterilisation is therefore advisable in winter or early spring.

Dichlorophen, quaternary ammonium compounds and tar acid/tar oil products are suitable as general disinfectants for application to greenhouse staging and structures, seed trays, pots, etc., to clean up algal slimes, moulds and other growths. This type of treatment is also useful as a general hygiene measure against grey mould *(Botrytis)* and tomato leaf mould. Sulphur used as a fumigant can also have a useful general disinfectant effect.

Tar acid/tar oil products, in addition to killing fungi, algae and other types of plant growth, kill numerous insect pests in their overwintering stages. They can also be used for soil sterilisation when applied by watering onto the soil or compost. This type of treatment helps to prevent the build-up of damping-off and foot rot diseases and, in addition, kills many soil pests, such as wireworms and woodlice.

Damping-off is a particular problem in germinating seeds and seedlings, whether in the greenhouse or outside, and Cheshunt compound based on copper sulphate applied as a soil drench provides protection though it will not cure plants which are already infected.

Fumigants

The enclosed nature of greenhouses makes it possible to apply chemicals by means of fumigation. Various pesticide chemicals are formulated in a solid, combustible form and, when such smoke cones are ignited, the chemical is dispersed in the smoke and penetrates into all the nooks and crannies of the structure. The broad-spectrum insecticides permethrin and pirimiphos-methyl are available in this form. A smoke cone formulation of the insecticide/fungicide mixture gamma-HCH + tecnazene can also be obtained. Permethrin is particularly effective against whitefly, a very common and persistent pest of greenhouses.

To use fumigation safely and effectively all greenhouse vents should be closed before applying the treatment and it is necessary to ensure that the roots of greenhouse plants are moist and their foliage dry. Fumigation is best done in the late afternoon or evening, not in strong sunlight. After the cones have been ignited the greenhouse should be kept closed for at least four hours, preferably overnight, and it must be ventilated thoroughly for at least one hour before re-entry. The chemicals used for fumigation are of short persistence and the treatment may need to be repeated to deal with such persistent pests as whitefly and red spider mite.

Another chemical particularly suited for use in confined spaces is dichlorvos which gives off an insecticidal vapour. When dichlorvos units are suspended in the greenhouse protection against most insect pests is provided for up to four months. Both with smoke cones and dichlorvos a few plant species may be affected by treatment and any instructions regarding susceptible species which should not be treated must be followed carefully.

Spray treatments

Many of the pest and disease problems and the chemicals used to combat them are basically the same in the greenhouse as outdoors and control recommendations may not make specific mention of greenhouse plants. With the products recommended for use on ornamentals or garden plants generally, however, the treatment should be suitable for greenhouse use as long as the label does not specifically exclude use on protected plants. Some of the disease problems of special importance in the greenhouse are listed below:

Grey mould
This disease is encouraged by high humidity. It can affect tomatoes, cucumbers, sweet peppers, grapevines and a wide range of ornamentals, including chrysanthemums, pelargoniums, etc. Control can be obtained by spraying as soon as the disease appears with benomyl, carbendazim or thiophanate-methyl.

Leaf mould
A disease of tomatoes encouraged by warm weather and high overnight humidity. It first appears as pale yellow patches on the leaves with a pale grey mould underneath which eventually becomes purplish. Good ventilation, especially around the lower leaves, helps to discourage the disease. If it makes an appearance, benomyl, carbendazim, mancozeb or thiophanate-methyl will provide control. Where the disease has been troublesome all plant material should be removed from the greenhouse and burnt at the end of the season and the house should be disinfected.

Powdery mildew
Grape powdery mildew is common on indoor vines in unheated green-houses and is encouraged by cold, wet weather, especially if the vines are dry at the roots. Sulphur applied as a spray or dust or in fumigant form is recommended for control. Benomyl or carbendazim can also be used but any treatment is likely to need repeating several times during the season.

31

Other types of powdery mildew affect a wide range of greenhouse plants. Benomyl or carbendazim are recommended for use on cucumbers and one of these chemicals, a bupirimate + triforine mixture or propiconazole can be used on many flowers and pot plants.

Sooty mould
This non-parasitic fungus forms a black, powdery deposit on the upper surface of leaves. It grows on the honeydew secreted by whitefly, aphids, scale insects and mealybugs. Control of these pests will prevent any further soiling of the foliage.

The common insect pests – greenfly, blackfly, capsids, caterpillars, leaf miners, thrips, etc. – cause trouble in the greenhouse as well as outdoors and similar treatments can be used for control. Pests of special importance in greenhouses include:

Fungus gnats
These small greyish-black gnats are commonly found running over the moist soil surface of pot plants. They are attracted to peaty composts and other organic matter and, although the adults are harmless, the maggots sometimes damage seedlings and young plants. Insecticides such as dichlorvos, gamma-HCH, permethrin and pirimiphos-methyl provide good control.

Mealybugs
These sucking insects are mainly pests of greenhouses and house plants. The adult female insects grow to about 5 mm across and have soft bodies covered by a fluffy, waxy deposit. They lay clusters of eggs, also enclosed in a waxy covering, and thrive under warm, humid conditions. Some species live in the soil and feed on plant roots. Small colonies can be killed by brushing spray-strength insecticide directly onto the pests with a paint brush. Spraying with dimethoate, malathion or pirimiphos-methyl is also effective but a soil drench must be used if the root feeding types are present.

Red spider mite
One of the worst greenhouse pests which is capable of attacking almost all types of plant. The first sign of an infestation is the appearance of a mottling of the upper surface of the leaves and the tiny mites (not necessarily red) are found on the underside. Severely infested leaves turn brown and die and a fine silky web appears over the plant. The mature females overwinter in cracks and crevices in the greenhouse structure and on plant remains. Careful attention to hygiene and a disinfectant treatment in winter will help to reduce problems in the following season. Pirimiphos-methyl is probably the most effective chemical but various other contact-acting insecticides, such as dimethoate, malathion and rotenone (derris) can be used for control. It is necessary to apply several treatments at

intervals of seven days or less. However, pesticide-resistant strains of glasshouse red spider mite can occur.

Scale insects
These are immobile, sap-feeding insects found on the undersides of leaves and on stems. Several species occur and they may be flat, oval, yellowish-brown or dark brown convex objects up to 5 mm long. Control by spraying with malathion or pirimiphos-methyl on two or three occasions at two-week intervals.

Whitefly
Another type of sap-feeding insect which is a very common problem on greenhouse plants of all kinds. The insects have the appearance of tiny white moths but they are more closely related to aphids. Normally they hide on the underside of the leaves but will fly about for short distances if disturbed. Like other sap-sucking insects, whitefly weaken the plants they feed on. Also the sticky honeydew they excrete during feeding commonly gives rise to the development of an unsightly black mould. Whitefly is susceptible to a number of sprays, including permethrin, pirimiphos-methyl or pyrethrum, but fumigation treatments are especially effective and convenient. Smoke cones based on permethrin, pirimiphos-methyl and the dual purpose gamma-HCH/tecnazene mixture are all available but several repeat treatments are normally needed to control successive hatches from the eggs. Some strains of whitefly have resistance to these insecticides but insecticidal soap sprays based on fatty acids can be effective against such resistant strains.

Soil treatments

The use of sterilised composts as media for growing plants in the greenhouse eliminates most of the common pests of garden soil such as wireworms and chafer grubs. Vine weevil, however, is common as a soil pest in pot plants. The adult beetles are flightless but often crawl into greenhouses and can also be introduced as eggs on plants brought in from outside. The grubs are white and legless and can do a considerable amount of damage as they destroy the root system on plants of many kinds. Once the damage is noticed it may be too late to save the plants but a measure of protection can be provided by drenching the compost with gamma-HCH or pirimiphos-methyl in July or early August.

Biological control

In commercial glasshouses extensive use of biological control is made against various pests, especially those which have developed resistance to chemical control. In particular, red spider mite can be controlled by a predatory mite, *Phytoseiulus* (**a**) and glasshouse whitefly by a parasitic wasp, *Encarsia* (**b**). These organisms are also available to the amateur gardener. Other beneficial insects which can be purchased include an Australian ladybird, *Cryptolaemus* (**c**), which feeds on mealybugs, mealybug parasites (**d**), a midge, *Aphidoletes (***e***)* whose larvae prey on aphids, and a small wasp, *Metaphycus* (**f**) which parasitises and kills scale insects. The micro-organism *Bacillus thuringiensis*, which infects and kills caterpillars, and the fungus *Trichoderma*, which combats silver leaf and dutch elm disease, are registered as pesticides and are included in the Pesticide Profiles section of the book.

In a successful biological control programme the introduced control organism builds up in numbers in the presence of the pest and, when established in sufficient numbers, reduces the infestation to an acceptably low level. However, this type of control cannot be expected to provide complete eradication. The insects mostly originate from the warmer parts of the world and are not well adapted to cool conditions. In unheated greenhouses, therefore, they should be used only from late April to September. They do not usually survive the winter. The insects are susceptible to the majority of insecticide chemicals (with the exception of pirimicarb which only kills aphids) and, if it is necessary to apply an insecticide treatment prior to using biological control, a chemical of short persistence should be selected.

Further details and supplies of the organisms can be obtained from:

English Woodlands Ltd., Grower Services Division, Graffham, Petworth, Sussex GU28 0LR (**a, b, c, e, f**).

Henry Doubleday Research Association, Ryton Court, Wolston Lane, Ryton-on-Dunsmore, Coventry CV8 3LG (**a, b, c, d, f**).

Natural Pest Control (Amateur), Watermead, Yapton Road, Barnham, Bognor Regis, W. Sussex PO22 0BQ (**a, b, c, e**).

Dr. M. Copland, Department of Biological Sciences, Wye College, University of London, Ashford, Kent TN25 5AH (**c, d, f**).

House plant chemicals

The pest and disease problems of house plants are generally similar to those associated with greenhouse plants. However, conditions in the home are normally very much drier than in greenhouses so that the diseases encouraged by warm, moist conditions are less prominent. The methods available for control are also similar, but additional care is needed to ensure the safety of the occupants of the house and of pets. The fumigation treatments so convenient for use in the greenhouse cannot normally be applied inside the home.

Generally only small numbers of house plants have to be treated and the plants themselves are often highly prized. It has, therefore, been found worthwhile for a number of products to be specially formulated and packaged for house plant use. Aerosol sprays and ready-to-use spray containers are particularly convenient for use in this situation.

Diseases

The commonest disease of a wide variety of house plants is powdery mildew, a problem encouraged by large fluctuations in temperature and humidity. It can be controlled by the use of benomyl or the combined fungicide/insecticide formulation based on dimethoate + gamma-HCH + thiram.

Pests

Insects commonly causing trouble include aphids, mealybugs, red spider mite, scale insects, thrips and whitefly. Contact insecticides based on pirimiphos-methyl, pyrethrum or the pyrethroid chemicals bioallethrin, permethrin and resmethrin can be used to obtain control. Care needs to be taken if there are fish tanks in the room where the plants are treated. Permethrin, in particular, is extremely dangerous to fish and should not be used in the presence of unprotected fish bowls or tanks. An alternative treatment which presents fewer toxic hazards is the soap concentrate spray based on fatty acids. Where fungus gnats are a problem pirimiphos-methyl is the recommended treatment. The combined dimethoate/gamma-HCH/thiram formulation contains both contact and systemic insecticides and deals with all the common insect pests as well as being an effective fungicide.

Two formulations of systemic insecticide designed to be taken up through the roots and subsequently distributed throughout the plant are particularly suitable for use on pot plants. One based on butoxycarboxim consists of chemically impregnated strips of card which release insecticide when inserted into moist soil. The other, also applied by insertion into moist soil, contains dimethoate mixed with a suitable house plant fertiliser and formulated as tablets.

A very wide range of plant species are grown as house plants and there is great variability in the degree of sensitivity to chemical treatment which they exhibit. With most chemicals a small number of subjects are liable to suffer damage and the product labels should be read carefully to find out which plants to avoid. Particular care should be taken with ferns. Most labels also warn against spraying open blooms or plants exposed to strong sunlight.

Non-crop weedkillers

Uncultivated ground

In the absence of cultivated plants there are few restrictions on the use of chemical weedkillers and the choice of product is based mainly on the types of weed to be controlled. However, if the aim of the treatment is just to kill off an existing cover of weeds on land which is later intended for sowing or planting, it is necessary to avoid the use of the more persistent soil-acting chemicals.

The least persistent products, both of which are non-selective, general purpose weedkillers, rapidly inactivated in contact with the soil, are the following:

Diquat + paraquat mixture

A fast-acting, rain-proof chemical which is effective against all types of annual weeds and grasses. Perennials, including couch grass, may be killed back to ground level but are likely to resprout and need repeated treatment.

Glyphosate

A slower acting chemical, the full effects of which may take several weeks to develop. However, in addition to annual weeds, it completely kills many perennials such as couch grass, in a single treatment. Rain falling within a few hours after treatment reduces its effects.

Some of the other weedkillers available are more specifically grass-killers, including:

Alloxydim-sodium

A chemical which kills most types of annual and perennial grass but has no effect on annual meadow grass or broad-leaved weeds. Some crops can be sown one day after application of this product but grass should not be sown for at least four weeks.

Dalapon

Also a grass-killer effective against most grass species, including annual meadow grass. It is more persistent than alloxydim-sodium and treated ground should be left for three months before planting.

Another chemical sometimes used as a general purpose weedkiller is:

Ammonium sulphamate

This is an inorganic salt which should not be confused with ammonium oulphate (sulphate of ammonia). It has a general use for killing weed growth in neglected gardens and a special use for killing unwanted troos and other woody weeds and preventing regrowth from cut stumps. It Is one of tho fow chemicals effective against rhododendron and its persistence is of the order of 8 – 12 weeks.

A number of other products are mixtures of translocated (systemic) chemicals which are moved within the plant from the leaves to the roots under suitable conditions. These products are used primarily for killing the more difficult perennial, broad-leaved weeds and include:

Aminotriazole + MCPA
This combination kills non-woody perennial weeds, such as nettles, thistles, docks and bindweed, together with some semi-woody species, including brambles and briars. Its soil persistence is of the order of three months.

2, 4–D + dicamba + mecoprop and dicamba + dichlorprop + MCPA
Triple mixtures which are also recommended for controlling broad-leaved perennials, brambles, brushwood and regrowth from tree stumps, etc. A period of at least six weeks should be allowed after treatment before planting.

Paths, drives and patios

In these areas it is not necessary for a weedkiller to be selective and long-term persistence is a desirable feature. Various single chemicals are available for non-selective use but, in order to combine a powerful killing action on established weeds with a long-lasting effect, it is generally necessary to combine chemicals with different modes of action in mixtures of various kinds.

Two widely used materials which act via the foliage and are effective in killing existing herbaceous growth but have no residual activity are:

Diquat + paraquat
A combination of two similar chemicals which is useful as a contact treatment. It provides a quick kill of annual weed growth but does not move far within the plant. Thus established perennial weeds normally resprout after treatment and regular re-treatment is needed to keep the area free of vegetation.

Glyphosate
A chemical with a mode of action quite different to that of diquat and paraquat. It not only kills the annual weeds but, being able to move extensively within the plant, is also effective against many perennials. Again, however, the lack of residual activity enables fresh weed infestations to become established as more seeds germinate.

Chemicals which act via the soil and have good residual activity but which have little or no effect via the foliage and so do not kill established weeds include:

Diuron and simazine
These weedkillers are from different chemical groups but they have a similar mode of action. They act via the soil and exert their effects mainly on germinating weed seedlings. Treatment with this type of chemical can prevent the establishment of weeds from seed for twelve months or more, depending on the rate of application. If established weed growth is present it must first be controlled with a contact weedkiller before using one of the residual chemicals.

Dichlobenil
Also a residual, soil-acting and persistent chemical. It kills weeds as they germinate but, unlike diuron and simazine, is also effective against many troublesome perennial weeds. Most woody plants, however, are not affected and the chemical does not move sideways in the soil (as long as it is not washed by water or soil movement) so that it can be applied safely up to the edges of paths and drives.

A few chemicals are active via the soil as well as being taken up through the foliage and combine persistence with a good effect on established weeds. Noteworthy among these is:

Sodium chlorate
A long-established general-purpose weedkiller which has been much used in gardens for non-selective weed control. It can be used on weed growth at any time of year but gives the best results in spring or early summer. A drawback is that it is highly soluble. Thus it can be leached through the soil and is liable to move sideways. Consequently it is not recommended for use near trees or shrubs, nor near to the edges of lawns and borders. Another disadvantage is that plant debris or clothing contaminated with the chemical becomes highly inflammable when it dries. Weedkillers based on sodium chlorate contain a fire-depressant as an additive but, even so, any clothing that becomes contaminated should be washed immediately.

Atrazine + sodium chlorate
A mixture marketed as a dust formulation in which extra persistence is provided by the addition of the atrazine. Precautions are the same as for sodium chlorate alone.

The translocated (or systemic) chemicals which are absorbed into plants through the leaves and then moved down into the underground parts are useful in weedkiller mixtures for uncultivated ground as they are effective against many deep-rooted perennial weeds. However, they are of relatively short persistence in the soil so that they are generally used in combination with one of the persistent soil-acting chemicals such as diuron or simazine. Apart from glyphosate, which has already been mentioned, commonly used translocated weedkillers are:

Aminotriazole
A non-selective chemical which affects both grasses and broad-leaved weeds. It has the characteristic feature that treated plants continue to grow for a while but the formation of chlorophyll is affected and the new growth is bleached or pinkish in colour.

Hormone weedkillers
A group of chemicals related to the naturally occurring plant growth hormones which includes 2, 4−D, dicamba, dichlorprop, MCPA and mecoprop. With all of these the effects develop slowly as the growth of the affected plants becomes twisted and distorted. They are effective against most types of broad-leaved weed but have little effect on grasses.

Mosses etc. on paths, drives and other hard surfaces

Mosses, algae and lichens on paths, drives and patios are unsightly and can also be dangerous as they make the surface slippery in wet weather. Similar growths are also liable to develop on walls and hard surfaces of all kinds. Such undesirable plant growth can be killed by an application of dichlorophen or a tar acid formulation but it is usually necessary to brush off the dead remains after a few days.

Moss killing products containing ferrous sulphate should not be used in this situation because of the risk of staining surfaces of brick, stone or concrete. Products containing fertiliser should also be avoided on hard surfaces as, not only is the fertiliser wasted, but it also encourages early reinfestation.

General chemicals

Slug and snail killers

Slugs and snails are normally present in gardens in large numbers and can cause a great deal of damage, especially to small seedlings. It is possible to keep down the numbers to some extent by controlling the rank grass and weed growth which shelter the snails and by cultivating the soil to expose slugs to the effects of predators and drying. Encouraging predators, such as hedgehogs, shrews, thrushes, etc., will also help to reduce the numbers, though rarely to a level where they no longer present a problem. For the protection of susceptible plants at critical periods of growth, therefore, it is often necessary to enlist the aid of chemical molluscicides.

The chemical most commonly used is metaldehyde. Slugs and snails affected by this pesticide are immobilized and produce large quantities of slime. They are killed by desiccation under dry conditions but may recover if it is wet. Metaldehyde is a toxic chemical which can be harmful to man, animals and birds as well as slugs and snails. Most of the products are formulated as small pellets which are coloured blue to discourage picking up by birds and also contain a deterrent to animals. Despite this, dogs are sometimes attracted to the pellets and can be killed if they pick up a sufficient quantity. It is, therefore, important to scatter the pellets thinly and not leave them in heaps on the soil surface. It goes without saying that they should be stored safely out of reach of children and pets.

As an alternative to metaldehyde, various products are available based on aluminium sulphate. This salt has a contact effect and can be applied as a dust or spray. It has the advantage of being much less toxic than metaldehyde or methiocarb. The latter is a third possibility which is both an insecticide and a molluscicide, killing various soil insects in addition to slugs and snails. Unlike the other two chemicals it is effective in wet conditions as well as in the dry.

Insecticides in the home

Many of the insecticides used against garden pests also have uses for insect control in and around the home. As would be expected, products formulated for domestic use are based on the chemicals of low mammalian toxicity. Domestic insecticides are intended primarily for use either against flying or crawling insects, though there is no hard and fast dividing line, and many products are equally effective against both.

Products for flying insects

For the control of flying insects (house and other flies, mosquitoes, midges,

wasps, moths, etc.) chemicals are needed which will kill rapidly by contact and have a 'quick knock-down' effect. For this purpose pyrethrum and related chemicals are very effective. Pyrethrum, a natural product extracted from the flowers of a cultivated species of *Chrysanthemum,* consists of a complex mixture of pyrethrins. It causes rapid paralysis of insects on contact and is non-persistent. It is generally formulated in conjunction with a synergist such as piperonyl butoxide which, although not itself an insecticide, greatly increases the activity of pyrethrins and related chemicals.

Various synthetic pyrethroid chemicals, chemically related to natural pyrethrins but with greatly increased activity, have also been produced. These include allethrin, bioallethrin and tetramethrin which have little persistence. Some other pyrethroids, such as cypermethrin and permethrin, have a greater degree of persistence and are thus more suitable for use in products to be sprayed on surfaces against crawling insects. Pyrethrum and the pyrethroids, although of relatively low toxicity towards mammals and birds, are highly toxic to fish. Other fast-acting contact chemicals suitable for use against flying insects in the home are fenitrothion and pirimiphos-methyl, two of the less toxic of the organophosphorus group of insecticides.

Most domestic flykillers consist of mixtures of the chemicals mentioned above and, for convenience, the majority are formulated as aerosols. Although the nature of the aerosol propellant is not generally disclosed on the label, it is understood that the great majority of products employ propellants of a non-CFC type (i.e. they are 'ozone friendly'). They are best used as space sprays, the aerosol being sprayed into the air in all directions for a few seconds in a closed room. They should not be sprayed directly onto food and any fish bowls or tanks should be covered or removed before spraying.

Products based on dichlorvos are used in a different way. The chemical volatilizes into the air when exposed and is active against pests in the vapour phase. It is formulated into blocks of different sizes which are suitable for use in different sized spaces and the spaces are cleared of insects when the blocks are exposed to the air. Some products are designed specifically for the control of clothes moths in wardrobes, drawers, etc.

Products for crawling insects

Formulations produced to control crawling pests may be effective by direct contact or as a deposit on surfaces. In the latter case insects are killed through foot contact as they crawl over the deposit. Most products combine both types of activity and many are dual purpose formulations intended for use against flying as well as crawling insects. An additional property, which is desirable in crawling insect killers and is characteristic of the pyrethroid chemicals, is the ability to flush insects out of their hiding places so that their exposure to the chemical is increased.

Certain chemicals are of particular value for use against crawling insects in situations where a long period of persistence is required. Carbaryl and gamma-HCH (lindane or gamma-BHC) are included for this purpose in a number of formulations. Chlordane has been used in the past but is now banned. Borax (boric acid, sodium tetraborate) is a persistent chemical of special use against ants. When formulated with sugar as a bait it is picked up by foraging ants and carried back to the nest where the grubs are killed in addition to the adults.

Aerosols and ready-to-use hand-operated sprayers are commonly used for applying crawling insect killers, the spray being directed onto suitable surfaces. Dust formulations are also suitable for surface application of residual chemicals and, with diazinon in particular, lacquer formulations provide another means of obtaining a persistent insecticidal deposit. These are applied onto non-absorbent surfaces where the insects are active and can be effective for up to six months. Cypermethrin can be used in a similar manner in the form of felt-tipped pens which deposit an invisible insecticidal line lasting for up to two weeks.

With the products applied as sprays it is necessary to take precautions to avoid the chemical entering fish tanks. With all types of surface application it is important to avoid contamination of any surfaces liable to come into contact with food. With those products used to control animal fleas in floors, floor coverings, pet bedding, etc., it must be appreciated that such products are not suitable for direct application to the pets themselves. Veterinary preparations for the control of animal parasites by direct application to the animals are not covered in this book.

Animal and bird repellents

At certain times of year birds can cause considerable damage to fruit, germinating seeds, seedlings and the buds of ornamental shrubs and trees. In rural areas moles can often be a problem in lawns and flower beds, while rabbits and occasionally deer can damage many kinds of garden plants. In all areas visits from cats and dogs can be unwelcome for a variety of reasons.

Physical barriers, such as effective fencing, netting of fruit bushes or the provision of a permanent fruit cage can often provide the most effective (though most costly) answer to such problems. Physical elimination by such means as trapping, etc., may also need to be considered on occasion. Less drastic psychological deterrents in the form of scarecrows, black cotton, windmills, kites in the shape of birds of prey and other devices can often afford a useful degree of protection for limited periods. Certain chemicals can also be used to deter unwelcome visitors and can be particularly useful when used in combination with other protective measures.

The chemicals used have little in common, apart from being disliked by animals and birds, and they are mostly materials which have been in use for many years.

The deterrent products are normally applied only to those parts of the plants likely to be attacked or to other localised targets, such as dog sniffing points. The treatment normally has to be re-applied at intervals, especially after rain, if long-term protection is required.

Rat, mouse and mole killers

Unlike the previous group of chemicals, rodenticides have been developed to kill, rather than repel, animal pests. As the chemicals are used for their ability to poison mammals it is only to be expected that they can also poison humans and pets. They are safe when used according to the directions but the precautionary statements printed on the packages of rat or mouse killer products must be read, understood and appreciated. It is essential that the directions are followed carefully.

In particular:

- Avoid all contact by mouth.
- Wash hands and exposed skin before meals and after use.
- Prevent access to baits by children and domestic animals, especially cats and dogs.
- Do not use where food or feed could become contaminated.
- Search for and burn or bury all rodent bodies.
- Remove all remains of bait and bait-containers after treatment and burn or bury them.
- Store unused sachets in a safe place.
- Do not store half-used sachets.

Some rodenticide products are effective against both rats and mice, others are intended for mice only. Formulations may vary depending on whether they are intended for use indoors or outdoors. Several of the chemicals act as cumulative poisons which must be eaten on several occasions before having the desired effects. With these, control may take up to two weeks. Others are effective in a single dose and work quicker. The products are mostly formulated as attractant baits on various types of grain. When applied, it will be found that a large number of smaller baits give better results than a few larger ones, especially for controlling mice. One product based on brodifacoum is formulated as a ready-to-use bait box and is thus especially convenient as no handling of the chemical is needed and the dangers of access by pets and children are minimised.

In some areas where older chemicals, such as warfarin, have been used regularly over a period 'super' rats and mice have developed which

have built up a resistance to the poison. In this situation it is necessary to use products containing one of the newer rodenticides, such as difenacoum, to obtain successful results.

Although they are not rodents it is convenient to include moles in this section. Non-chemical methods are more commonly used for their control in gardens but sulphur can also be an effective treatment. In the form of 'mole smokes' the chemical is ignited and inserted into the mole tunnels. The toxic gas sulphur dioxide is given off and either kills or repels the moles as well as any rats or mice using the same tunnels.

CHEMICALS AVAILABLE FOR USE

Index to sections

A Crop Chemicals

AA Crop insecticides

AA 1	Bacillus thuringiensis
AA 2	bioallethrin + permethrin
AA 3	borax
AA 4	borax + carbaryl
AA 5	bromophos
AA 6	carbaryl
AA 7	carbaryl + rotenone (derris)
AA 8	(chlordane)
AA 9	dichlorvos + gamma-HCH + tetramethrin
AA 10	dimethoate
AA 11	dimethoate + permethrin
AA 12	fatty acids
AA 13	fenitrothion
AA 14	gamma-HCH (BHC, lindane)
AA 15	gamma-HCH + pyrethrum
AA 16	grease
AA 17	heptenophos + permethrin
AA 18	malathion
AA 19	malathion + permethrin
AA 20	permethrin
AA 21	phoxim
AA 22	pirimicarb
AA 23	pirimiphos-methyl
AA 24	pirimiphos-methyl + pyrethrins
AA 25	pyrethrins/pyrethrum
AA 26	pyrethrins/pyrethrum + resmethrin
AA 27	pyrethrum + rotenone (derris)
AA 28	quassia + rotenone (derris)
AA 29	rotenone (derris)
AA 30	tar acids/tar oils (cresylic acid)

AB Crop fungicides

AB 1	benomyl
AB 2	bupirimate + triforine
AB 3	carbendazim
AB 4	copper oxychloride
AB 5	copper sulphate
	(a) copper sulphate + ammonium carbonate
	(b) copper sulphate + ammonium hydroxide
	(c) copper sulphate + calcium hydroxide
AB 6	mancozeb
AB 7	mercurous chloride (calomel)
AB 8	myclobutanil
AB 9	propiconazole
AB 10	pyrazophos

AB 11   sulphur
AB 12   thiophanate methyl
AB 13   Trichoderma viride

AC Crop fungicide/insecticide mixtures

AC 1   bupirimate + pirimicarb + triforine
AC 2   captan + gamma-HCH
AC 3   carbendazim + copper oxychloride + permethrin + sulphur
        with fertiliser
AC 4   dimethoate + gamma-HCH + thiram
AC 5   dinocap + permethrin + sulphur + triforine with fertiliser
AC 6   gamma-HCH + rotenone (derris) + thiram
AC 7   rotenone (derris) + sulphur
AC 8   tar acids/tar oils (cresylic acid)

AD Crop weedkillers

AD 1   alloxydim-sodium
AD 2   ammonium sulphamate
AD 3   dalapon
AD 4   dicamba + MCPA + mecoprop
AD 5   dichlobenil
AD 6   diquat + paraquat
AD 7   glyphosate
AD 8   propachlor
AD 9   simazine

AE Pruning wound products

AE 1   bitumen
AE 2   tar acids/tar oils (cresylic acid)
AE 3   wax

AA Crop insecticides

AA 1 Bacillus thuringiensis

A bacterial insecticide active against caterpillars.

1 Atlas Thuricide HP	Atlas	WP	02087
2 Bactospeine Garden	Koppert	WP	02913
3 Dipel	English Woodlands	WP	03214

Control of caterpillars of cabbage butterfly and cabbage moth on brassicas and of various caterpillars on other vegetables and ornamentals.

Spray as soon as caterpillars appear and repeat treatment as necessary. Product must be eaten by caterpillars to be effective and good coverage is essential.

AA 2   bioallethrin + permethrin

A mixture of fast-acting, contact pyrethroids

see also under **Greenhouse insecticides** (CA), **House plant chemicals** (D), **Domestic insecticides** (GA, GB)

1 Boots Kill-A-Bug Spray Gun	Boots	RH	03957
2 Spraydex Greenfly Killer	Spraydex	RH	04847

Control of greenfly, blackfly, whitefly, caterpillars, red spider mite and most common insect pests on fruit, flowers, vegetables, roses and ornamental shrubs [1], on flowers and vegetables [2].

Apply ready-to-use spray at first sign of pest attack and repeat as necessary. Spray in calm conditions and avoid direct sunlight. Do not use on begonias, ferns, vines or succulents. Do not spray open flowers or immature leaves.

Fruit and vegetables are best left unpicked for 24 hours after spraying. Dangerous to bees. Extremely dangerous to fish.

AA 3   borax (sodium tetraborate)

A mineral insecticide particularly effective against ants

see also under **Domestic insecticides** (GA)

1 Nippon Ant Killer Liquid	Synchemicals	LB	01502
2 Rentokil Ant Killer	Rentokil	LB	04312

Control of ants in the home and garden.

Place a few drops of product on a piece of flat wood, glass or metal where ants run; chemical is then carried back to the nest. Best applied late in the evening. Repeat treatment as necessary. Activity is destroyed by rain.

AA 4   borax + carbaryl

A mixture of borax ant killer with a general purpose insecticide

see also under **Domestic insecticides** (GA)

Boots Ant Killer	Boots	DP	04088

Control of ants, woodlice and soil pests, including wireworms, cutworms, leatherjackets, cabbage root fly and flea-beetles, in the home and garden.

For control of ants and woodlice apply indoors or outside where pests are active and at the entrance to nests. For soil pests apply to surface and rake in. May need to be re-applied after heavy rain.

Do not apply near crops other than brassicas, peas, lettuce or tomatoes. Do not gather food crops within seven days of treatment. Dangerous to bees; do not dust crops in open flower.

AA 5 bromophos

A contact and stomach-acting organophosphorus insecticide

see also under **Greenhouse insecticides** (CA)

1 PBI Bromophos	PBI	GR	00340
2 Spring Spray	Synchemicals	EC	02006

Control of soil pests, including cutworms, wireworms, chafer grubs, onion fly, carrot fly and cabbage root fly [1], and as a pre-bud burst spray on fruit trees, soft fruit, roses, ornamental shrubs and conifers to control overwintering pests [2].

For control of soil pests sprinkle granules around base of brassica seedlings and other plants immediately after planting or rake into surface before sowing or planting [1]. For control of overwintering pests apply a drenching spray to cover all surfaces (including the ground beneath plants) before bud-burst or emergence of needles. Do not spray young emerging leaves.

Do not pick food crops within seven days of treatment.

AA 6 carbaryl

A contact and stomach-acting carbamate insecticide and worm killer

see also under **Lawn insecticides** (BA), **Wormkillers** (BE), **Domestic insecticides** (GA).

1 Dethlac Ant & Insect Powder	Gerhardt	DP	03584
2 Rentokil Ant & Insect Powder	Rentokil	DP	01755
3 Rentokil Wasp Nest Killer	Rentokil	DP	01786

Control of ants, cockroaches, silverfish and other crawling insects in the home and of ants, blackfly, caterpillars, earwigs, flea-beetles, greenfly, sawflies and other insects in the garden [1, 2]. Control of wasps [3].

Apply dust indoors where pests are active [1, 2]. Dust soil, grass or plants outside where pests are seen [1, 2]. For wasp control, dust liberally inside entrance to nest, preferably in the evening when wasps are not flying [3].

Dangerous to bees.

AA 7 carbaryl + rotenone (derris)

Carbaryl plus a non-persistent contact insecticide

Boots Garden Insect Powder with
Derris	Boots	DP	02849

Control of caterpillars and other leaf feeding insects (aphids, capsids, sawflies, blossom weevils, beetles, etc.) and soil pests (including carrot fly, flea-beetles, earwigs, cutworms, leatherjackets,

etc.) in fruit and vegetable crops and ornamentals. Also for control of wasps.

Dust over plants as soon as pests seen and repeat treatment as necessary. See label for details of timing on fruit. Dust may also be applied to soil or turf. For wasp control apply liberally in nest entrance in the evening.

Do not gather food crops within seven days of treatment. Dangerous to bees; do not dust crops in open flower.

AA 8 (chlordane)

A persistent organochlorine insecticide approvals for home and garden use of which were revoked at the end of 1988. It is no longer legal to stock this chemical for sale to amateur gardeners. It is also illegal for amateur gardeners to store or use chlordane. Any gardeners with remaining stocks of this chemical should consult the local authority waste disposal department for advice on disposal. (Nippon Ant Powder, which contained chlordane, has been replaced by a new formulation based on permethrin).

derris – see **rotenone**

AA 9 dichlorvos + gamma-HCH + tetramethrin

An insecticide mixture combining fumigant, ingested and fast knock-down contact activity

see also under **Greenhouse insecticides** (CA)

Secto Aphid Killer	Secto	AE	03704

Control of greenfly, blackfly, whitefly, caterpillars, leafhoppers, leaf miners, red spider mite, thrips and many other pests of flowers, fruit and vegetables.

Spray as soon as pests first observed and repeat treatment as necessary.

AA 10 dimethoate

A systemic organophosphorus insecticide and acaricide

see also under **House plant chemicals** (D)

1	Boots Greenfly and Blackfly Killer	Boots	EC	02402
2	Doff Systemic Insecticide	Doff	EC	02658
3	Murphy Systemic Insecticide	Fisons	EC	03636

Control of greenfly, blackfly, capsid bugs, leafhoppers and other sucking insects (including red spider mite and whitefly [3]) on roses, most flowers and vegetables [1, 2], on fruit trees, roses, most flowers and vegetables [3].

Spray at first signs of infestation and repeat after 3–4 weeks as necessary. For whitefly control repeat every seven days [3]. May also be applied by soil watering for greenfly control on roses [3]. Do not use on chrysanthemums, or flowering cherries [1, 3], nor on decorative hops [1], or on asters, salvias or sage [2, 3].

AA 11 dimethoate + permethrin

Dimethoate plus a contact-acting and residual pyrethroid insecticide

see also under **Greenhouse insecticides** (CA)

1 Bio Long Last	PBI	EC	00269
2 Secto Systemic Garden Insect Killer Concentrate	Secto	LI	02950

Control of foliar pests, including ants, greenfly, blackfly, woolly aphid, beetles, capsid bugs, caterpillars, earwigs, flea beetles, froghoppers, leafhoppers, leaf miners, maggots, midges, red spider mite, sawflies, scale insects, slugworm, suckers, thrips, weevils, whitefly and woodlice on flowers, fruit, vegetables and ornamental trees and shrubs.

Apply as a spray at first signs of attack and repeat as necessary. Do not use on chrysanthemums, asters or salvias.

Do not harvest edible crops within 14 days after last spray.

AA 12 fatty acids

A contact-acting, soap concentrate insecticide

see also under **Greenhouse insecticides** (CA), **House plant chemicals** (D)

1 Bio Friendly Pest Pistol	PBI	RH	04911
2 Safer's Fruit & Vegetable Insecticide	Phostrogen	RH	04329
3 Safer's Rose & Flower Insecticide	Phostrogen	RH	04341
4 Savona	Koppert	SL	03137

Control of insect pests, such as aphids, earwigs, leafhoppers, mealybugs, red spider mite, scale insects, sawflies, slug sawfly, thrips, whitefly, etc. on outdoor flowers, shrubs, fruit and vegetables [1], on fruit, vegetables, pot plants, roses and other shrubs [2 – 4].

Spray thoroughly, using ready-to-use spray [1, 2, 3], or diluted as directed (preferably with soft water) [4], at first signs of pest attack and repeat as necessary. For control of whitefly spray every two weeks.

AA 13 fenitrothion

A contact-acting, organophosphorus insecticide

1	Murphy Fentro	Fisons	LI	00859
2	PBI Fenitrothion	PBI	SC	01552

Control of greenfly, blackfly, caterpillars, leafhoppers, capsid bugs, raspberry beetle and other insect pests of flowers, fruit and vegetables.

Apply as spray when pests are first seen and repeat as necessary. For control of codling moth and sawfly on apples and pears spray at petal-fall, mid-June and early July. For control of raspberry beetle spray as soon as fruit begins to turn pink [2]. For control of pea moth spray 7–10 days after first flowers open. Do not spray open blooms.

Do not gather food crops within fourteen days of spraying; allow seven days with raspberries [2].

AA 14 gamma-HCH (BHC, lindane)

A contact and stomach-acting organochlorine insecticide

see also under **Domestic insecticides** (GA)

1	5% BHC Horticultural Dust	B.H. & B.	DP	01078
2	Cuton Ant Powder	Cramphorn	DP	04211
3	Doff Ant Killer	Doff	DP	00739
4	Gamma-BHC Garden Spray	B.H. & B.	WP	00963
5	Murphy Ant Killer Powder	Fisons	DP	03614
6	Murphy Gamma-BHC Dust	Fisons	DP	00962
7	Soil Insecticide Powder	B.H. & B.	DP	01977

Control of ants [2, 5], ants, aphids, beetles, caterpillars, and other crawling insects [1, 4], of cabbage root fly, carrot fly, onion fly, cutworms, leatherjackets, wireworms, chafer grubs and other soil pests [6, 7], in the garden. Control of ants and other crawling insects in the home and garden [3].

For control of ants apply dust along runs and in nests. For control of pests on crops dust or spray as appropriate when pests first seen and repeat as necessary. For timing of sprays on fruit trees see label [4]. For control of soil pests apply dust to surface and work into soil before sowing or planting; apply along seedling rows for control of flea beetle, carrot and onion flies; apply around base of plants for control of cabbage root fly [6, 7]. Do not treat blackcurrants, cucumbers, grapevines, marrows, potatoes or hydrangeas.

Do not gather food crops within fourteen days of treatment.

AA 15　gamma-HCH + pyrethrins/pyrethrum

Gamma-HCH plus a quick-acting, contact pyrethrum product

see also under **Domestic insecticides** (GA, GC)

1 Ant Killer	B.H. & B.	DP	00100
2 Secto Extra Strength Ant Killer Powder	Secto	DP	00816
3 Secto Greenfly and Garden Insect Spray	Secto	RH	03843
4 Secto House & Garden Powder	Secto	DP	01901
5 Secto Insect Killer Powder	Secto	DP	01902
6 Secto Wasp Killer Aerosol	Secto	AE	01911

Control of ants, beetles, earwigs and other crawling insects in the home and garden [1, 2, 4, 5], of greenfly, blackfly, whitefly, caterpillars and other insect pests on garden plants [3, 4], control of wasps [6].

Sprinkle powder indoors or outdoors into places where pests are active [1, 2, 4, 5]. Apply ready-to-use spray or dust onto garden plants when pests are first seen and repeat treatment as necessary [3, 4]. Apply aerosol spray in and around entrance to wasp nest, preferably in the evening.

Dangerous to bees. Do not treat plants in open flower.

AA 16　grease

High viscosity mineral oil product used to trap insects crawling up tree trunks

1 Corry's Fruit Tree Grease	Synchemicals	GS	00583
2 PBI Boltac Greasebands	PBI	GS	00288

Control of winter moth and March moth caterpillars and other crawling insects on fruit trees.

Brush on trunk or apply grease bands above the level of the grass or surrounding plants in winter and renew in spring or summer if necessary. Grease must form a complete ring about 10 cm wide around the trunk. Tree stake should also be treated if present.

AA 17　heptenophos + permethrin

A systemic organophosphorus and contact-acting pyrethroid insecticide mixture

see also under **Greenhouse insecticides** (CA)

Murphy Tumblebug	Fisons	LI	03637

Control of all foliar insect pests (ants, greenfly, blackfly, whitefly, capsid bugs, caterpillars, earwigs, leafhoppers, leaf miners, mealybug, pea moth, raspberry beetle, sawflies, scale insects, suckers, thrips, etc.) on fruit, flowers and vegetables.

Apply as spray when pests first seen and repeat as necessary. See label for details of timing.

AA 18 malathion

A contact-acting organophosphorus insecticide and acaricide

see also under **Greenhouse insecticides** (CA)

1 Greenfly Aerosol Spray	B.H. & B.	AE	01002
2 Malathion Dust	B.H. & B.	DP	01241
3 Malathion 50 Liquid Spray	B.H. & B.	LI	01249
4 Murphy Liquid Malathion	Fisons	LI	01248
5 Murphy Malathion Dust	Fisons	DP	01244
6 PBI Malathion Greenfly Killer	PBI	LI	01247

Control of greenfly, blackfly, whitefly, capsid bugs, leafhoppers, mealybug, red spider mite, thrips, and other insect pests (including scale insects and woolly aphid [4, 6]) on fruit, flowers and vegetables.

Apply when pests first seen and repeat at fourteen day intervals if necessary. Do not treat antirrhinum, crassula, ferns, petunia, sweet pea or zinnia.

Dangerous to bees; do not spray plants in open flower. Do not pick food crops within four days of treatment [1, 4, 5], three days [2, 3], one day [6].

AA 19 malathion + permethrin

Malathion plus a contact-acting pyrethroid insecticide

PBI Crop Saver	PBI	SC	03969

Control of greenfly, blackfly, whitefly, capsid bugs, caterpillars, earwigs, flea beetles, leafhoppers, leaf miners, thrips and other pests of vegetable crops.

Apply at first signs of pest attack and repeat as necessary.

Allow at least one day after spraying before picking vegetables.

AA 20 permethrin

A contact-acting pyrethroid insecticide with good residual activity

see also under **Greenhouse insecticides** (CA), **House plant chemicals** (D), **Domestic insecticides** (GA)

1 Bio Sprayday	PBI	EC	00272
2 Boots Caterpillar & Whitefly Killer	Boots	EC	00290
3 Picket	ICI	EC	01590

Control of caterpillars, whitefly, greenfly, blackfly, capsid bugs, leafhoppers, pea maggots, raspberry beetle, sawflies, suckers and other leaf-feeding insect pests (also cutworms and leatherjackets [2]) on fruit, flowers and vegetables.

Spray plants thoroughly when pests first seen, as soon as eggs laid if possible, and repeat as necessary (every 7–14 days for whitefly

control). For details of timing on fruit crops see label. For cutworm and leatherjacket control apply to soil surface [2]. Do not spray in bright sunlight.

Crops may be picked and eaten on the same day as spraying. Dangerous to bees; do not spray plants in open flower. Extremely dangerous to fish; avoid drift into fish ponds.

AA 21 phoxim

A contact-acting organophosphorus insecticide for soil pests

1	Fisons Antkiller	Fisons	DP	00873
2	Fisons Soil Pest Killer	Fisons	GR	00893
3	Murphy Kil-Ant	Fisons	DP	03965

Control of ants, earwigs, woodlice and other crawling insect pests outdoors [1, 3], of wireworms, cutworms, chafer grubs, cabbage root fly, carrot fly, millipedes and other soil pests [2].

Dust entrance to nests and along runs frequented by ants etc.; do not apply over plants [1, 3]. Sprinkle granules on soil before sowing or around the base of transplants [2]. Repeat after 6–8 weeks if necessary.

Dangerous to bees, birds and fish.

AA 22 pirimicarb

A systemic, non-persistent, specific aphid killer

see also under **Greenhouse insecticides** (CA)

1	Rapid Aerosol	ICI	AE	01689
2	Rapid	ICI	EC	01690

Control of greenfly, blackfly, woolly aphid and other aphids on fruit, vegetables and ornamental plants [2], on roses and other flowers [1].

Apply at first signs of pest attack and repeat as necessary. Do not apply in bright sunlight. Do not use on cucumbers or other cucurbits. Do not use aerosol spray on open flowers, cacti or other succulents [1]. Bees and other beneficial insects, such as ladybirds and lacewings, are not affected.

Do not gather lettuce grown under glass within fourteen days after treatment or other food crops within three days.

AA 23 pirimiphos-methyl

An organophosphorus insecticide and acaricide with fast-acting contact and fumigant activity

see also under **Lawn insecticides** (BA), **Greenhouse insecticides** (CA)

1	ICI Antkiller	ICI	DP	00101
2	Sybol	ICI	EC	02058
3	Sybol Dust	ICI	DP	03494

Control of ants, earwigs, wasps and woodlice in the garden, greenhouse and home [1], of greenfly, blackfly, whitefly, cabbage root fly, capsid bugs, caterpillars, earwigs, flea-beetles, leafhoppers, leaf miners, pea moth, pea and bean weevil, red spider mite, sawflies and thrips on fruit, flowers and vegetables [2], of cabbage root fly, carrot fly, onion fly, wireworm, flea beetles, caterpillars, chafer grubs and other soil pests in vegetables [3].

Dust powder along runs in and around ant and wasp nests [1], on soil surface along seed drills and on and around plants [3]. Spray at first signs of pest attack and repeat at seven day intervals where necessary (four day intervals for whitefly) [2]. See label for further details. Do not treat celery or cucurbits; do not treat strawberries or raspberries after flowering.

Do not gather food crops within seven days after treatment. Treat flowering plants only in evening when bees have stopped working. Avoid drift of chemical over fish ponds.

AA 24 pirimiphos-methyl + pyrethrins

As previous entry with addition of pyrethrins for formulation as an aerosol

see also under **Greenhouse insecticides** (CA), **House plant chemicals** (D), **Domestic insecticides** (GA, GB)

| Sybol Aerosol | ICI | AE | 03597 |

Uses and precautions as for Sybol in previous entry [AA 23.2].

AA 25 pyrethrins/pyrethrum

Non-persistent, contact insecticides of natural origin, based on extracts of pyrethrum flowers

see also under **Greenhouse insecticides** (CA), **House plant chemicals** (D), **Domestic insecticides** (GA, GB)

1	Bio Friendly Anti-Ant Duster	PBI	DP	00098
2	Bug Gun for Fruit and Vegetables	ICI	RH	03076
3	Bug Gun for Roses and Flowers	ICI	RH	03076
4	Doff Fruit & Vegetable Insecticide Spray	Doff	RH	04040
5	Doff Rose & Flower Insecticide Spray	Doff	RH	04041
6	Gateway Pest Spray for Fruit & Vegetables	Sinclair	RH	03985

7 Gateway Pest Spray for Roses & Flowers	Sinclair	RH	03986
8 Py Garden Insecticide	Synchemicals	AE	02811
9 Py Powder	Synchemicals	DP	02809
10 Py Spray Garden Insect Killer	Synchemicals	LI	02810

Control of ants indoors and outdoors [1]. Control of greenfly, blackfly, whitefly, capsid bugs, caterpillars, leafhoppers, thrips and other insect pests on fruit and vegetables [2, 4, 6], on roses and flowers [3, 5, 7], on garden plants [8–10]. Control of wasps [8–10].

Apply spray or dust as appropriate when pests first seen and repeat at 4–7 day intervals as necessary. Ensure both upper and lower surfaces of leaves are covered. Some varieties of hydrangea, dahlia and crassula may be sensitive [8–10]. Do not spray open blooms or flowers in direct sunlight.

May be used on food crops up to day of harvest [2], up to one day before harvest [4, 7, 9, 10], up to three days before harvest [6].

AA 26 pyrethrins/pyrethrum + resmethrin

Pyrethrum plus a powerful, non-persistent contact-acting pyrethroid insecticide

see also under **Greenhouse insecticides** (CA), **House plant chemicals** (D)

1 Doom Garden Insect Killer Aerosol	Napa Products	AE	00747
2 Doom Greenhouse & Garden Insect Killer	Napa Products	AE	02694
3 Rentokil Blackfly & Greenfly Killer	Rentokil	AE	02984
4 Rentokil Greenhouse & Garden Insect Killer	Rentokil	AE	02983

Control of greenfly, blackfly, whitefly, red spider mite and many other insect pests on roses, flowers, fruit crops and vegetables.

Apply aerosol spray sparingly at first signs of pest attack and repeat as necessary. Do not spray closer than 30 cm (1 ft) or in bright sunshine. Do not spray open blooms.

AA 27 pyrethrum + rotenone (derris)

A mixture of contact insecticides of natural origin

Greenfly Spray	B.H. & B.	SL	01003

Control of greenfly, blackfly, other aphids, ants, caterpillars and other insect pests on flowers, fruit and vegetables.

Spray when pests first seen, ensuring that both lower and upper leaf surfaces are covered, and repeat as necessary.

Do not pick food crops within one day of treatment. Dangerous to fish; do not allow drift of spray over fish ponds.

AA 28 quassia + rotenone (derris)

A mixture of insecticides of natural origin.

see also under **Greenhouse insecticides** (CA)

Bio Friendly Insect Spray   PBI   SL   00180

Control of greenfly, blackfly, caterpillars and many other garden pests.

Dilute as directed, spray when pests first seen and repeat treatment as necessary.

AA 29 rotenone (derris)

A natural insecticide of short persistence extracted from roots of Derris and related plants

see also under **Greenhouse insecticides** (CA)

1 Derris Dust	B.H. & B.	DP	00672
2 Derris Dust			
(ex Corry's Derris Dust)	Synchemicals	DP	00676
3 Doff Derris Dust	Doff	DP	00740
4 ICI Derris Dust			
(ex Abol Derris Dust)	ICI	DP	02651
5 Murphy Derris Dust	Fisons	DP	00674
6 PBI Liquid Derris	PBI	EC	01214
7 Wasp Exterminator	B.H. & B.	DP	02342

Control of greenfly, blackfly, caterpillars, raspberry beetle, sawflies, flea beetle, red spider mite, thrips and other insect pests on fruit, flowers and vegetables [1–6]. Especially useful on soft fruit. Control of wasps [5, 7].

Apply dust (or spray [6]) at first signs of pest attack and repeat as necessary. For flea beetle control apply at four day intervals until seedlings established. See label for details of timing on fruit crops. Apply powder liberally at entrance to wasp nests and repeat after seven days if necessary [5, 7].

Do not pick food crops within one day of treatment. Dangerous to fish; do not allow drift over fish ponds.

AA 30 tar acids/tar oils (cresylic acid)

Tar distillates used as winter washes and with various other uses

see under Crop fungicide/insecticide mixtures (AC 8)

see also under **Pruning wound chemicals** (AE), **Lawn chemicals** **(BC, BD), Greenhouse disinfectants** (CD), **Non-crop mosskillers** (EB)

AB Crop fungicides

AB 1 benomyl

A broad-spectrum, protective and curative systemic fungicide

see also under **Lawn fungicides** (BB), **Greenhouse fungicides** (CB), **House plant chemicals** (D)

Benlate + Activex   ICI   WP 02491

Prevention and control of powdery mildew, black spot, grey mould and other diseases on roses and flowers (including pot plants), of powdery mildew, grey mould, leaf spot, scab and other diseases on soft fruit and fruit trees, of moulds, stem rot, wilts, leaf spots, chocolate spot and other diseases on tomatoes, broad beans and other vegetables.

Apply as a protective spray at fourteen day intervals during the period when disease is likely to occur (warm, humid conditions) or as a curative spray when the first signs of disease appear, repeating the treatment at 10–14 day intervals as necessary. Include Activex with all spray treatments. May also be used as a soil drench before planting out tomatoes or pricking out seedlings, as a dip to protect bulbs and corms against storage rots and in powder form (without Activex) as a seed treatment against seed and soil-borne diseases.

Harvest interval zero; may be applied up to and during harvest. Harmless to beneficial insects but may be mixed with an insecticide (Sybol, Picket or Rapid) for pest control.

AB 2 bupirimate + triforine

A preventive and curative systemic fungicide mixture

Nimrod T   ICI   LI 01499

Prevention and control of mildew, black spot and rust on roses and other flowers, mildew and scab on apples, mildew and leaf spot on blackcurrants and gooseberries.

Apply spray at 10–14 day intervals, starting in May for roses, at bud-burst for apples and at first flowering for blackcurrants and gooseberries. Spray in calm conditions and not in bright sunlight.

Do not gather apples within seven days of treatment, blackcurrants or gooseberries within fourteen days.

AB 3 carbendazim

A broad-spectrum protective and curative systemic fungicide

see also under **Lawn fungicides** (BB), **Greenhouse fungicides** (CB)

1 Boots Garden Fungicide   Boots   SC 02401
2 PBI Supercarb   PBI   WP 03891

Prevention and control of powdery mildew, black spot and other diseases on roses and flowers (including pot plants), of powdery mildew, grey mould, leaf spot, scab and other diseases on soft fruit and fruit trees, of moulds, leaf spots, blight, chocolate spot and other diseases on vegetables.

Spray at the first signs of disease and repeat three times at fourteen day intervals. Spray flower bulbs and corms as the growing point emerges or use as a dip before planting. Apples and pears can also be dipped before storage. Do not spray during hot conditions or on plants suffering from drought.

Food crops can be eaten safely the same day as spraying, except for lettuce where a fourteen day interval should be left before spraying and eating.

AB 4   copper oxychloride

A general purpose, protective copper-based fungicide

Murphy Traditional Copper Fungicide	Fisons	WP	04585

Control of damping off and foot rot of seedlings, blight on potatoes and outdoor tomatoes, rust and leaf spot on currants and gooseberries, cane spot on raspberries and other cane fruit, peach leaf curl and bacterial canker on plums and cherries.

To control damping off, water onto compost after sowing, pricking out or potting up. For control of diseases on potatoes, tomatoes, currants and gooseberries, spray thoroughly at first signs of disease and then every fourteen days, for other fruit diseases see label for details.

Keep away from fish.

AB 5   copper sulphate

see also under **Greenhouse fungicides** (CB)
(a) **copper sulphate + ammonium carbonate**

A fungicide mixture protecting against damping off

1 Cheshunt Compound	B.H. & B.	SP	00484
2 PBI Cheshunt Compound	PBI	SP	00485

Prevention of damping off in germinating seeds and seedlings of all types.

Dissolve in warm water and thoroughly wet compost at sowing, after seedling emergence and before or after transplanting. Not effective on plants already infected. Remove all dead or diseased plants. Do not mix in metal containers.

(b) **copper sulphate + ammonium hydroxide**

A general purpose, protective fungicide mixture

Spraydex General Purpose
    Fungicide   Spraydex   RH   02865

Control of rose mildew and black spot, chrysanthemum mildew, tomato and potato blight, raspberry cane spot, gooseberry mildew, apple and pear scab.

Apply as ready-to-use spray at first signs of disease and repeat as necessary.

(c) **copper sulphate + calcium hydroxide** (Bordeaux mixture)

A mixture protecting against blight and many other fungus diseases

| 1 | Bordeaux Mixture | B.H. & B. | SP | 00296 |
| 2 | Bordeaux Mixture | Synchemicals | SP | 00297 |

Control of blight on potatoes and tomatoes, leaf curl on peaches and nectarines, leaf spot and rust on blackcurrants, gooseberries and celery, canker on apples, plums and cherries and many other diseases of garden plants.

May be applied as a dust but better as a spray. Apply when conditions conducive to disease (usually in late summer) and repeat every 2–4 weeks. See label for details of timing.

AB 6   **mancozeb**

A protective fungicide containing zinc and manganese trace elements for control of blight and many other diseases

see also under **Greenhouse fungicides** (CB)

Dithane 945   PBI   WP   00718

Control of blight on potatoes and tomatoes. of black spot, rust, mildew, apple and pear scab, peach leaf curl and many other diseases of garden plants.

Apply spray at first signs of disease or otherwise as directed on the label and repeat every 7–14 days. Agitate container while spraying to prevent settling out.

Do not harvest food crops for seven days after application or with lettuce, for 21 days.

AB 7   **mercurous chloride** (calomel)

A mercury based fungicide for application to the soil

1	Calomel Dust	B.H. & B.	DP	00376
2	Doff Calomel Dust	Doff	DP	00371
3	ICI Club Root Control	ICI	DP	00548
4	PBI Calomel Dust	PBI	DP	02551

Control of club root in cabbages, cauliflowers, turnips and other brassicas (also stocks and wallflowers) and of white rot in onions.*

Apply dust to seed drills and rake in lightly before sowing. At transplanting, dust roots of plants and planting holes or, alternatively, mix into a paste with water and dip the roots.

Keep away from fish.

AB 8 myclobutanil

A broad-spectrum, curative and protective systemic fungicide

1 PBI Systhane	PBI	WP	04523
2 Systhane	Rohm & Haas	WP	04522

Control of black spot, mildew and rust on roses.

For mildew and low risk black spot or rust situations apply at first signs of disease and repeat every fourteen days. For high risk situations spray when leaves begin to open in spring (black spot), or at first signs of disease (rust), and repeat after seven days. Continue routine spraying every fourteen days.

AB 9 propiconazole

A systemic fungicide for use on ornamental plants

Murphy Tumbleblite	Fisons	LI	02471

Control of black spot, rust and mildew on roses, of antirrhinum rust and of mildew on begonias, chrysanthemums, Michaelmas daisy and other flowers.

Spray when first signs of disease appear and repeat as necessary.

Dangerous to fish. Do not use on food crops or on fuchsias.

AB 10 pyrazophos

A systemic fungicide active against mildew

Pokon Mildew Spray	Chrysal	AE	01610

See entry under **House plant chemicals** (D)

AB 11 sulphur

A non-systemic protective fungicide for control of mildew and various other diseases

see also under **Greenhouse chemicals** (CD)

1 Green Sulphur	Synchemicals	DP	01007
2 Green Sulphur Powder	B.H. & B.	DP	01008
3 Safer's Garden Fungicide	Koppert	RH	03539

---

* Footnote: In accordance with EEC requirements mercurous chloride may only be recommended for use against club root in brassicas and white rot in onions.

4 Safer's Garden Fungicide	Phostrogen	RH	04342
5 Yellow Sulphur	Synchemicals	DP	02372
6 Yellow Sulphur Powder	B.H. & B.	DP	02373

Control of powdery mildew on most fruit, flowers and vegetables [1, 5], mildew on strawberries, gooseberries and peas, powdery mildew on vines and peaches, apple scab and mildew, downy mildew on roses and chrysanthemum rust [2, 6], black spot, powdery mildew and rust on fruit, ornamentals and vegetables [3, 4]. Also for protection of bulbs, corms, tubers and fruit during storage [1, 5], of dahlia tubers [2, 6].

Sprinkle dust evenly or apply ready-to-use spray as a protective treatment.

Do not use on red or white currants, sulphur-shy apples (Beauty of Bath, Belle de Boskoop, Cox's Orange Pippin, Lane's Prince Albert, Lord Derby, Newton Wonder, Rival, Stirling Castle) or sulphur-shy gooseberries (especially Leveller).

AB 12 thiophanate-methyl

A broad-spectrum protective and curative systemic fungicide

see also under **Lawn fungicides** (BB), **Greenhouse fungicides** (CB)

| 1 M&B Liquid Club Root Control | May&Baker | SC | 01211 |
| 2 M&B Systemic Fungicide Liquid | May&Baker | SC | 00952 |

Control of club root in brassicas [1], of powdery mildew and grey mould on flowers, fruit and vegetables, black spot on roses, apple and pear scab, apple canker, spur blight and cane spot on cane fruit, leaf spot on currants and gooseberry and various other fungus diseases [2].

Apply as a root dip or soil drench for club root control [1]. For other diseases spray to wet foliage thoroughly at first signs of disease and repeat treatment as required [2].

Food crops can be eaten on the same day as spraying.

AB 13 Trichoderma viride

A fungal agent providing biological control of certain tree diseases

| Binab T | HDRA | WP, PT | 00264 |

Prevention and control of silver leaf disease on plums, other Prunus and certain other trees. Control of Dutch elm disease.

Mix wettable powder with water and paint or spray onto tree wounds for prevention and control of silver leaf. Bore holes into trunk and insert pellets for control of Dutch elm disease. See label for details.

AC Crop fungicide/insecticide mixtures

AC 1 bupirimate + pirimicarb + triforine

A systemic mixture of two fungicides and an aphid-killer

Roseclear   ICI   LI   01826

Prevention and control of mildew and black spot on roses and other ornamentals, of mildew and scab on apples, mildew and leaf spot on blackcurrants and gooseberries, combined with control of greenfly and blackfly.

Spray at 10–14 day intervals, starting in April for roses, at bud-burst for apples, at first flowering for blackcurrants and gooseberries. Aphids are killed within 30 minutes, other pests and beneficial insects are not harmed. Do not spray in bright sunlight.

Irritating to the eyes. Do not pick apples within seven days, blackcurrants and gooseberries within fourteen days of last spray.

AC 2 captan + gamma-HCH

A mixture of a non-systemic fungicide and an organochlorine insecticide

Murphy Combined Seed Dressing Fisons   DS   03893

Prevention of seed rot, damping off and footrot, combined with control of carrot fly, flea beetle, wireworm and other soil insects in sown flowers and vegetables.

Mix powder with seed and sprinkle in seed drill at sowing. Do not use on onion, mangold or beet seed, or on seeds sown in boxes or pans, use sparingly on antirrhinum or lettuce seed.

AC 3 carbendazim + copper oxychloride + permethrin + sulphur with fertiliser

A mixture of three fungicides and a contact pyrethroid insecticide plus a leaf-absorbed fertiliser

Bio Multiveg   PBI   WP   03116

Control of blight, botrytis (grey mould), chocolate spot, damping off, powdery mildew and other diseases, of blackfly, greenfly, caterpillars, cutworms, whitefly and other insect pests on vegetable crops, combined with promotion of growth.

Spray when pests or disease first seen and repeat every fourteen days as required.

Allow fourteen days after last spray before picking lettuce; no restriction for other vegetable crops.

AC 4 dimethoate + gamma-HCH + thiram

A mixture of systemic and contact insecticides and acaricides with a protective fungicide

see also under **Greenhouse chemicals (CC), House plant chemicals** (D)

1 Secto Garden Powder	Secto	DP	02774
2 Secto Rose & Flower Spray	Secto	RH	03843

Control of greenfly, blackfly, whitefly, caterpillars, sawflies, leafhoppers, leaf miners, raspberry beetle, thrips, red spider mite and other pests, and of black spot, downy mildew, moulds and other diseases on ornamentals, vegetables, tomatoes and raspberries [1], on roses and other flowers [2].

Apply by dusting or as ready-to-use spray when pests first seen and repeat as required.

AC 5 dinocap + permethrin + sulphur + triforine with fertiliser

A mixture of three fungicides and a contact-acting pyrethroid insecticide plus a foliar feed

Bio Multirose	PBI	WP	02541

Control of black spot, mildew, greenfly, caterpillars and other insect pests of roses combined with growth promotion.

Spray for black spot control in early spring, for other pests and diseases when first seen, and repeat every fourteen days as necessary.

AC 6 gamma-HCH + rotenone (derris) + thiram

A mixture of two insecticides and a protective fungicide

PBI Hexyl	PBI	WP	02650

Control of many insect pests (ants, aphids, capsid bugs, caterpillars, cuckoo-spit, earwigs, leaf miners, sawflies, weevils, red spider mite) and fungus diseases (black spot, downy mildew, leaf mould, rust, scab) on flowers, fruit, vegetables, trees and shrubs.

Apply as spray at first signs of pest or disease attack and repeat as necessary, every 10–14 days for disease control. Do not spray hydrangeas, vines, cucumbers, marrows, young tomatoes, beetroot, potatoes or soft fruit.

Do not harvest edible crops for fourteen days after last spray.

AC 7 rotenone (derris) + sulphur

A mixture of natural insecticide and fungicide

see also under **Greenhouse chemicals** (CD)

Bio Friendly Pest & Disease Duster	PBI	DP	00265

Control of blackfly, greenfly, caterpillars, mildew and many other pests and diseases all round the garden.

Apply at first signs of pest or disease attack and repeat treatment as necessary.

AC 8   **tar acids/tar oils** (cresylic acid)

Tar distillates used as general purpose sterilising agents

see also under **Crop chemicals** (AA, AE), **Lawn chemicals** (BC, BD), **Greenhouse chemicals** (CD), **Non-crop mosskillers** (EB)

1 Clean-up	ICI	EC	00539
2 Jeyes Fluid	Jeyes	EC	04606
3 Murphy Mortegg	Fisons	EC	03616
4 Tar Oil Winter Wash	B.H. & B.	EC	02087

Control of overwintering pests (aphids, apple sucker, scale insects, mealybugs) and diseases and cleaning of bark on fruit trees, bush and cane fruit, grapevines and roses [1–4], including ornamental Prunus and Malus [1].

Apply a coarse spray as a winter wash when plants fully dormant, from December to February. Do not apply when buds starting to open in spring or before buds fully brown in autumn. Avoid drift and protect surrounding plants and grass to avoid scorch.

Keep off skin. Wash off splashes of concentrate immediately. Do not breathe spray mist.

AD   Crop weedkillers

AD 1   **alloxydim-sodium**

A selective, translocated grass killer

M & B Weed Out	May & Baker	SG	04531

Control of couchgrass amongst growing ornamental plants (not ornamental grasses).

Spray evenly over infested area, ensuring that grass weeds are thoroughly wetted. Best applied when grass has adequate leaf area and is growing actively.

Irritating to eyes and skin.

AD 2   **ammonium sulphamate**

A solid, crystalline salt used as a non-selective weedkiller

see also under **Non-crop weedkillers** (EA)

1 Amcide	B.H. & B.	CR	00089
2 Dax Root-Out	Dax	CR	03510

Control of annual and many perennial weeds (not bracken) in new and neglected gardens before replanting and killing of unwanted trees, shrubs (including rhododendron) and tree stumps.

For general weed control dissolve in water, add detergent and apply as foliage spray in dry weather during growing season (April to October). For woody weed control cut stems near ground and spray regrowth, or apply crystals in frill cut or on stump. See label for details. Only use plastic or stainless steel sprayers and mixing vessels to avoid corrosion. Do not spray ground covering the roots of valuable trees or shrubs. Treated areas can be planted safely 8–12 weeks after treatment.

AD 3   dalapon

A translocated grass weed killer

see also under **Non-crop weedkillers** (EA)

Synchemicals Couch & Grass
    Killer   Synchemicals   SP   02735

Control of couch and many other grass weeds among apples, pears, blackcurrants and gooseberries at least three years old and in asparagus, raspberries and rhubarb.

Spray in spring or autumn using a protected nozzle to avoid contact with the crop or turf, see label for details of timing in different crops. Apply only sufficient spray to wet grass foliage thoroughly and avoid run-off. Do not spray in frost or drought. Delay sowing or planting sensitive crops (e.g. grass seed, peas, beans, onions and brassicas) for at least twelve weeks after treatment.

AD 4   dicamba + MCPA + mecoprop

A mixture of hormone weedkillers

see also under **Non-crop weedkillers** (EA)

Bio Weed Pencil   PBI   AL   04054

Control of broad-leaved weeds by spot treatment in rose beds, rockeries, walls and other hard-to-treat areas.

Invert bottle and squeeze gently to prime sponge pad. Apply by dabbing onto the centre and leaves of individual weeds. Re-treat as necessary.

AD 5   dichlobenil

A residual, soil-acting weedkiller

see also under **Non-crop weedkillers** (EA)

Casoron G4   Synchemicals   GR   00450

Control of annual weeds and suppression of perennials, including docks, nettles, field horsetail, creeping thistle, willowherb, ground elder and couchgrass, among established roses, certain ornamental trees and shrubs, apples, pears and bush fruit.

Sprinkle granules evenly over the soil before spring growth starts (February or early March). All plants must have been established for at least two years. Do not apply to frozen or waterlogged soil, when plant foliage wet, to areas underplanted with bulbs or to herbaceous plants. Do not disturb untreated soil. Do not apply near greenhouses.

Store well away from bulbs, corms, tubers and seeds.

AD 6 diquat + paraquat

A non-selective, non-persistent, general purpose contact-acting weedkiller

see also under **Non-crop weedkillers** (EA)

Weedol	ICI	SG	02357

Control of annual weeds, grasses and top growth of perennials between crop rows, around plants, on seedbeds before sowing or before emergence of crop seedlings. Also for ground clearance prior to cultivation, as well as on non-crop areas, and may be used to kill unwanted young suckers of roses and some other shrubs.

Dissolve granules in water as directed and apply with ICI Applicator or a watering can fitted with a sprinkler bar or fine rose, preferably when the weeds are small. Wet weed foliage thoroughly but take care to keep solution off plants, especially small seedlings, and lawns. May be used up to the base of trees and shrubs but avoid low-growing buds and immature green stems or bark. Chemical is inactivated on contact with soil but do not use on pure peat or peat/sand composts, which may not fully inactivate the chemical. Rain falling soon after treatment does not reduce efficacy. In bulbs, asparagus, etc. only use after the plant foliage has completely died back and been removed; plant crowns must be covered by soil.

AD 7 glyphosate

A non-selective, non-residual translocated weedkiller

see also under **Lawn weedkillers** (BC), **Non-crop weedkillers** (EA)

1	Greenscape Weedkiller	Monsanto	SL	04321
2	Murphy Ready-to-Use Tumbleweed Sprayer	Fisons	RH	01458
3	Murphy Tumbleweed	Fisons	SL	01456
4	Murphy Tumbleweed Gel	Fisons	PA	01457

Control of most types of weed between garden plants and on uncultivated ground.

Apply as a light spray [2], with a sprayer or a watering can fitted with a fine rose or sprinkler bar [1, 3], with the brush provided [4], on a dry day from spring to autumn. Take care to avoid contact with garden plants, including lawn grasses. Repeat treatment if rain falls within six hours. Perennials may need retreatment if they resprout. Treated ground can be used for planting or sowing as soon as weeds have died. Do not use galvanised or mild steel watering cans or sprayers. Crops can be planted the day after treating a light cover of annual weeds; allow seven days after treating a dense cover which includes perennial weeds.

AD 8 propachlor

A residual, soil-acting weedkiller for control of annual weeds

No Weed   Arable & Bulb   GR   01507

Control of annual weeds (including annual meadow grass, chickweed, cleavers, groundsel, shepherd's purse and speedwell) in certain sown and transplanted vegetables, strawberries, annual bedding plants, established flowers, shrubs and trees. See label for detailed list.

Apply to soil immediately after sowing or planting or at other times as recommended on label. Established weeds are not controlled and must be removed before application. Hoeing after application reduces efficacy. Do not apply in very wet or windy conditions.

AD 9 simazine

A residual, soil-acting weedkiller

see also under Non-crop weedkillers (EA)

Murphy Weedex   Fisons   WP   02352

Control of annual weeds in roses, conifers, certain trees and shrubs (see label for list of sensitive species), apples, pears, currants, gooseberries, cane fruit, strawberries, rhubarb, asparagus and sweetcorn.

Apply to weed-free soil in early spring, in strawberries from July to November, to rhubarb in early spring or autumn, to sweetcorn within seven days of sowing. Do not exceed dose recommended for selective weed control. All treated plants (except sweetcorn) should have been established for at least twelve months. Only make one application per year. Do not disturb the soil after treatment.

Do not sow any other crop for at least seven months after application.

AE Pruning wound products

AE 1 **bitumen**

A wound sealant based on bitumen emulsion

PBI Arbrex   PBI   PA   —

Protection of wounds and pruning cuts from pests and diseases and promotion of callus formation.

Paint onto cut surfaces, allow to dry and apply second coat. Use only in good drying conditions when frost not expected. May be mixed with sand to fill cavities.

AE 2 **tar acids/tar oils** (cresylic acid)

Tar distillates used as general purpose sterilizing agents

see also under **Crop chemicals** (AA, AC), **Lawn chemicals** (BC, BD), **Non-crop mosskillers** (EB)

Medo (ex Corry's Medo)   Synchemicals   EC   02073

Protection of wounds and pruning cuts against infection and as a canker paint on fruit and other trees.

Apply to wounds and canker sites with a stiff brush, working well into cracks and crevices. Do not apply to green or very young bark.

AE 3 **wax**

A soft, brush-on mineral wax formation

Tenax Wax (ex Corry's)   Synchemicals   PA   —

Sealing and protection of pruning cuts and wounds and for use as grafting wax.

Apply to form waterproof and airtight seal over cut tissues.

B Lawn Chemicals

BA Lawn insecticides
BA 1   carbaryl
BA 2   carbaryl with fertiliser
BA 3   pirimiphos-methyl

BB Lawn fungicides
BB 1   benomyl
BB 2   carbendazim
BB 3   dichlorophen
BB 4   dichlorophen with fertiliser
BB 5   thiophanate-methyl

BC Lawn weedkillers
BC 1   benazolin + 2, 4–D + dicamba + dichlorophen +
         dichlorprop + mecoprop with fertiliser
BC 2   2, 4–D with fertiliser
BC 3   2, 4–D + dicamba
BC 4   2, 4–D + dicamba with fertiliser
BC 5   2, 4–D + dicamba + ferrous sulphate with fertiliser
BC 6   2, 4–D + dichlorprop
BC 7   2, 4–D + dichlorprop with fertiliser
BC 8   2, 4–D + dichlorprop + mecoprop
BC 9   2, 4–D + ferrous sulphate with fertiliser
BC 10   2, 4–D + ferrous sulphate + mecoprop with fertiliser
BC 11   2, 4–D + mecoprop
BC 12   2, 4–D + mecoprop with fertiliser
BC 13   2, 4–D + 2, 3, 6–TBA
BC 14   dicamba + dichlorprop + MCPA
BC 15   dicamba + dichlorprop + MCPA with fertiliser
BC 16   dicamba + MCPA
BC 17   dicamba + MCPA + mecoprop
BC 18   dicamba + MCPA + mecoprop with fertiliser
BC 19   dichlorprop + ferrous sulphate + MCPA with fertiliser
BC 20   dichlorprop + MCPA with fertiliser
BC 21   ferrous sulphate with fertiliser
BC 22   glyphosate
BC 23   MCPA + mecoprop with fertiliser
BC 24   tar acids/tar oils (cresylic acid)

BD Lawn mosskillers
BD 1   benazolin + 2, 4–D + dicamba + dichlorophen +
         dichlorprop + mecoprop with fertiliser
BD 2   chloroxuron + dichlorophen + ferrous sulphate with fertiliser
BD 3   chloroxuron + ferric sulphate with fertiliser
BD 4   chloroxuron + ferrous sulphate
BD 5   2, 4–D + dicamba + ferrous sulphate with fertiliser

BD 6	2, 4–D + ferrous sulphate + mecoprop with fertiliser
BD 7	dichlorophen
BD 8	dichlorophen with fertiliser
BD 9	dichlorophen + ferrous sulphate with fertiliser
BD 10	dichlorprop + ferrous sulphate + MCPA with fertiliser
BD 11	ferrous sulphate
BD 12	ferrous sulphate with fertiliser
BD 13	tar acids/tar oils (cresylic acid)

BE   Lawn wormkillers

BE 1	benazolin + 2, 4–D + dicamba + dichlorophen + dichlorprop + mecoprop with fertiliser
BE 2	carbaryl
BE 3	carbaryl + fertiliser
BE 4	(chlordane)

BA   Lawn insecticides

BA 1   carbaryl

A contact and stomach acting carbamate insecticide and wormkiller

see also under **Crop insecticides** (AA), **Lawn wormkillers** (BE), **Domestic insecticides** (GA)

Murphy Lawn Pest Killer   Fisons   SC   04433

Controls chafer grubs, leatherjackets, ants and worms in lawns.

Apply by sprayer or watering can in April and/or September or when pests active. Control lasts for up to six months. Mow before treatment. After treatment, if mowing needed before a good rain has fallen, mow without grass box. Later mowings may be composted.

BA 2   carbaryl with fertiliser

A carbamate insecticide and wormkiller combined with a high phosphate, low nitrogen fertiliser

see also under **Lawn wormkillers** (BE)

PBI Autumn and Winter Toplawn   PBI   GR   04138

Control of leatherjackets and worms combined with strengthening the grass roots.

Apply evenly by hand or lawn spreader from September to April or when preparing to sow or turf new lawns.

BA 3   pirimiphos-methyl

A general purpose organophosphorus insecticide with contact and fumigant action

see also under **Crop insecticides** (AA), **Greenhouse insecticides** (CA)

Sybol   ICI   EC   02058

Control of chafer grubs, leatherjackets and other insect pests in lawns.

Apply as a drenching spray during autumn or spring under humid weather conditions.

BB   Lawn fungicides

BB 1   benomyl

A protective and curative systemic fungicide

see also under **Crop fungicides** (AB), **Greenhouse fungicides** (CB), **House plant fungicides** (D)

Benlate + Activex   ICI   WP   02491

Control of fusarium patch, red thread and dollar spot diseases in lawns.

Mix ingredients as directed, add water and spray thoroughly as soon as signs of disease appear. Shake spray mixture during use to prevent settling out. Repeat at 10–14 day intervals as necessary.

BB 2   carbendazim

A protective and curative systemic fungicide

see also under **Crop fungicides** (AB), **Greenhouse fungicides** (CB)

1 Boots Garden Fungicide   Boots   SC   02401
2 PBI Supercarb   PBI   WP   03981

Control of fusarium patch, red thread and dollar spot diseases in lawns.

Mix as directed and spray at first signs of disease. Repeat three times at fourteen day intervals. Do not spray during hot, droughty conditions.

BB 3   dichlorophen

A phenolic mosskiller, fungicide and algae killer

see also under **Lawn mosskillers** (BD), **Greenhouse chemicals** (CD), **Non-crop mosskillers** (EB)

| 1 Algofen | Geeco | SL | 02392 |
| 2 Bio Moss Killer | PBI | SL | 00270 |

Control of mosses, turf diseases, toadstools and mushrooms.

Apply with sprayer or watering can when disease appears and repeat as necessary.

BB 4 **dichlorophen with fertiliser**

A mosskiller and fungicide combined with a nitrogen + phosphorus fertiliser

see also under **Lawn mosskillers** (BD)

| Boots Spring and Autumn Lawn Treatment | Boots | WP | 03628 |

Control of turf diseases and fairy rings together with lawn feeding.

Apply evenly with a watering can in spring and autumn. Use a higher rate of application against fairy rings. Do not mow for four days before or after treatment. Do not treat when frost or rain likely within four hours.

BB 5 **thiophanate-methyl**

A broad-spectrum protective and curative systemic fungicide

see also under **Crop fungicides** (AB, AE), **Greenhouse fungicides** (CB)

| M&B Systemic Fungicide Liquid | May & Baker | SC | 00952 |

Control of fusarium patch, red thread and dollar spot disease in lawns.

Spray thoroughly at first signs of disease and repeat treatment as necessary.

BC Lawn weedkillers

BC 1 **benazolin + 2, 4–D + dicamba + dichlorophen + dichlorprop + mecoprop with fertiliser**

A mixture of contact and hormone weedkillers, and a mosskiller combined with nitrogen and potassium fertiliser

see also under **Lawn mosskillers** (BD), **Lawn wormkillers** (BE)

| Boots Total Lawn Treatment | Boots | SL | 00293 |

Control of most lawn weeds, moss and worms and promotion of grass growth.

Mix as directed and apply by sprayer or watering can between March and October under warm, still conditions. Do not mow for four days before or after treatment. Do not apply in drought or

when frost or rain likely within four hours. Repeat after twelve weeks if necessary. Speedwell is checked but not eliminated.

Do not treat new lawns for six months. Do not compost the first mowing after treatment. Avoid spray drift over plants or shrubs.

BC 2   2, 4–D with fertiliser

A hormone weedkiller combined with nitrogen, phosphorus and potassium fertiliser

Notcutts Granular Lawn Feed & Weed	Notcutt's	GR	04045

Control of most broad-leaved weeds (not speedwell or clovers) and promotion of grass growth.

Apply in spring when grass starts to grow and repeat treatment 4–6 weeks later. Soil should be moist but surface dry. Water in after 48 hours. Grass seed may be sown 30 days after second application.

Do not use first two mowings after treatment for compost. Avoid drift onto flowers, shrubs and all cultivated crops.

BC 3   2, 4–D + dicamba

A mixture of hormone weedkillers

1 Bio Lawn Weedkiller	PBI	SL	00268
2 Fisons Lawn Spot Weeder	Fisons	AE	00886
3 Green-up Weedfree Lawn Weedkiller	Synchemicals	EC	02942
4 Green-up Weedfree Spot Weedkiller	Synchemicals	AE	03253
5 Weed Gun for Lawns	ICI	RH	03077

Control of daisies, buttercups, dandelions, plantains and most other common lawn weeds.

Apply by watering can [1], by watering can or sprayer [3], apply ready-to-use spray to single weeds or small patches [5], direct foam onto individual weeds as a spot treatment [2, 4]. Apply on a calm day between April and September when soil moist and weeds growing vigorously. Do not mow for three days before or after treatment. Repeat after six weeks if necessary [1], three weeks [3, 4]. Do not use on lawns established for less than six months.

Keep off garden plants. Do not use first mowing after treatment for compost or mulch.

BC 4   2, 4–D + dicamba with fertiliser

A mixture of hormone weedkillers combined with a nitrogen, phosphorus and potassium fertiliser

1 Green-up Lawn Feed & Weed	Synchemicals	SL	02897
2 Lawnsman Weed & Feed	ICI	GR	02535
3 Oak Lawnmaster Lawn Feed with Weedkiller	Oak	GR	04501
4 PBI Toplawn	PBI	GR	02145

Control of broad-leaved lawn weeds and promotion of grass growth.

Apply with a watering can or sprayer [1], by hand or with a lawn spreader [2–4], between April and September under calm conditions, when soil moist and weeds actively growing. Do not mow for three days before or after treatment (four days after [2]). Water thoroughly if no rain falls within 48 hours after treatment [2, 4]. Do not apply on newly sown lawns.

Avoid drift onto garden plants. Do not use first mowings for compost or as a mulch.

BC 5 2, 4–D + dicamba + ferrous sulphate with fertiliser

A hormone weedkiller/mosskiller mixture combined with a nitrogen, phosphorus and potassium fertiliser

see also under **Lawn mosskillers** (BD)

| Triple Action Grasshopper | ICI | GR | 03932 |

Control of daisies, dandelions, self-heal, white clover, other broad-leaved lawn weeds and moss and promotion of grass growth.

Apply with applicator provided at any time from April to September when grass leaves dry and soil moist. For best results mow 3–4 days before applying and allow 4–5 days afterwards. Water thoroughly if no rain falls within a few days after applying. Applicator may be re-used in conjunction with refill packs. Difficult weeds, such as black medick, speedwell, yarrow and yellow suckling clover may need a follow-up treatment with Verdone 2 after 4–5 weeks.

Do not treat lawns sown or turfed for less than six months. Do not use clippings from first four or five mowings as a fresh mulch.

BC 6 2, 4–D + dichlorprop

A mixture of hormone weedkillers

| 1 Doff Lawn Spot Weeder | Doff | RH | 03995 |
| 2 Doff Lawn Weedkiller | Doff | SL | 01187 |

Control of most common broad-leaved lawn weeds, including buttercups, daisies, dandelions, hawkbit, hawksbeard, plantains, self-heal, sorrel, thistles, white clover and yarrow.

Apply as a spot spray [1], with a sprayer or watering can [2], between April and September, on a fine day when soil is moist. Persistent weeds may need a repeat treatment 4–6 weeks later. Do not mow for three days before or after treatment. Keep spray away from garden plants.

BC 7 2, 4-D + dichlorprop with fertiliser

A mixture of hormone weedkillers combined with urea nitrogen fertiliser

Murphy Lawn Weedkiller and Lawn Tonic	Fisons	SL	03619

Control of broad-leaved lawn weeds and promotion of grass growth.

Apply with a watering can or sprayer between April and September (June and July best for clover and trefoils) when weeds are growing actively, not in drought or just before rain. Do not mow for three days before or after treatment. Repeat after four weeks if necessary. Do not use on lawns established for less than 6–9 months.

Keep off garden plants. Do not use first mowings after treatment as mulch.

BC 8 2, 4-D + dichlorprop + mecoprop

A mixture of three hormone weedkillers

1 Boots Kill-A-Weed	Boots	RH	03523
2 Boots Lawn Weedkiller	Boots	SL	02677

Control of daisies, buttercups, dandelions, plantains, clovers, chickweed, sorrel and most common lawn weeds.

Apply with a watering can or sprayer [2], as a spot treatment [1], between May and August, when weeds growing vigorously and rain not expected for a few hours. Do not apply during drought. Do not mow for four days before or after treatment. Repeat after 4–6 weeks if necessary. Do not use on lawns sown less than six months previously.

Avoid drift onto garden plants. Do not compost grass cuttings from first mowing after treatment.

BC 9 2, 4-D + ferrous sulphate with fertiliser

A mixture of a hormone weedkiller with iron and an organic nitrogen, phosphorus and potassium fertiliser

see also under **Lawn mosskillers** (BD)

Good Life Lawn Weed & Feed	Humber	GR	04242

Control of broad-leaved lawn weeds and promotion of grass growth.

Apply evenly on a calm day when the grass is dry, but not during drought. Mow before applying. Water thoroughly if no rain falls within 24 hours. Do not apply any other herbicide within three weeks.

BC 10   2, 4–D + ferrous sulphate + mecoprop with fertiliser

A hormone weedkiller/mosskiller mixture combined with a nitrogen, phosphorus and potassium fertiliser

see also under **Lawn mosskillers** (BD)

1 ASDA Lawn Weed & Feed + Mosskiller	ASDA	GR	03819
2 Gem Lawn Weed & Feed + Mosskiller	Gem	GR	04488
3 Green-up Feed & Weed + Mosskiller	Synchemicals	GR	04450
4 M&B Supergreen Feed, Weed & Mosskiller	May & Baker	SP	03884
5 Vitax Weed'N'Feed Extra	Vitax	GR	03450

Control of broad-leaved lawn weeds and moss and promotion of grass growth.

Apply granules evenly on a still day in early spring and repeat in June or July [1–3, 5], when weeds growing actively between April and September using a watering can [4]. Apply 2–3 days before or after mowing [1, 2], mow three days before treatment and not again for at least four days after [3]. Water in if no rain falls for 48 hours; do not apply to wet grass or during drought; avoid walking on treated areas until chemical has been washed in [1–3, 5].

Do not use first three mowings as mulch until composted for six months. Do not use on sown or laid grass until established for at least twelve months.

BC 11   2, 4–D + mecoprop

A mixture of hormone weedkillers

1 Concentrated Selective Weed Killer	B.H. & B.	SL	00567
2 Gateway Weedspray for Lawns	Sinclair	RH	03787
3 M&B Lawn Spot Weed Granules	May & Baker	GR	04028
4 M&B Supertox Lawn Weed Spray	May & Baker	SL	02049
5 Spraydex Lawn Spot Weeder	Spraydex	RH	03141
6 Verdone 2	ICI	SL	03271
7 Verdone 2 Spot Weeder	ICI	AE	03272

Control of most broad-leaved lawn weeds.

Apply as an overall treatment with a sprayer or watering can fitted with a fine rose [1, 4, 6], or as a spot treatment, using granules [3], ready-to-use spray [2, 5] or as aerosol foam [7] between April and

September, when the soil is moist and the weeds growing vigorously. Do not mow for three days before or after treatment. Repeat treatment after 4–6 weeks if necessary. Do not treat new lawns for 6–9 months after sowing or 3–4 months after turfing.

Do not use first mowings after treatment for mulching.

BC 12   2, 4–D + mecoprop with fertiliser

A mixture of hormone weedkillers combined with a nitrogen, phosphorus and potassium fertiliser

1	ASDA Lawn Weed & Feed	ASDA	GR	03721
2	Gateway Lawn Feed with Weedkiller	Sinclair	SL	04303
3	Gem Lawn Weed & Feed	Gem	GR	04486
4	Gem Lawn Weed & Feed 4	Gem	GR	04487
5	J Arthur Bowers Lawn Food with Weedkiller	Sinclair	SL	04301
6	M & B Lawn Feed & Weed Granules	May & Baker (granules based on organic lignite)	GR	04525
7	M & B Supergreen & Weed	May & Baker	SL	02570
8	Payless Lawn Weed & Feed	Gem	GR	03722
9	Proctors Lawn Weed & Feed	Proctor	GR	04669
10	Wilko Lawn Feed'N'Weed	Sinclair	GR	04403
11	Wilko Lawn Food with Weedkiller	Sinclair	SL	04302

Control of broad-leaved lawn weeds and promotion of grass growth.

Apply evenly with an appropriate applicator on a still day when the weeds are growing vigorously, in early spring and again in June or July [3, 4], from April to September [6, 7]. Apply 2–3 days before or after mowing and, with granules, water if no rain falls within 48 hours. Do not apply more than three times per year [3, 4]. Do not use on new lawns established for less than twelve months.

Do not use first three mowings for mulch until composted for at least six months. Keep off garden plants.

BC 13   2, 4–D + 2, 3, 6–TBA

A mixture of hormone weedkillers

Pocket Touchweeder	Elliott	WX	02864

Control of buttercups, daisies, dandelions, plantains and other broad-leaved lawn weeds by spot treatment.

Smear lightly on the centres of the weeds at any time during the growing season. Repeat after 2–3 weeks if necessary.

Do not touch garden plants or shrubs.

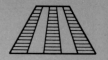

BC 14 dicamba + dichlorprop + MCPA

A mixture of three translocated hormone weedkillers

Boots Nettle & Bramble
Weedkiller   Boots   SL   03455

Control of perennial broad-leaved weeds in rough grass.

see entry under **Non-crop weedkillers** (EA)

BC 15 dicamba + dichlorprop + MCPA with fertiliser

As former entry with addition of nitrogen (ammonium nitrate and urea) fertiliser

Lawnsman Liquid Weed & Feed   ICI   SL   03610

Control of broad-leaved lawn weeds and promotion of grass growth.

Apply with a watering can or special applicator at any time between April and September when the weeds are growing vigorously. Do not mow for three days before or after treatment. Repeat the treatment after 4–6 weeks if necessary. Do not use on lawns established for less than 6–9 months.

First mowings should be well composted before being used as mulch. Keep off garden plants.

BC 16 dicamba + MCPA

A mixture of hormone weedkillers

Fisons Turf Weeds Killer   Fisons   SL   03235

Control of most broad-leaved turf weeds.

Apply evenly with a watering can fitted with a fine rose or a sprinkler bar on a calm, fine day at any time between April and late September when the soil is moist. Do not mow for three days before or after treatment. Repeat after 4–6 weeks if necessary. Do not use on lawns under six months old.

Compost the first three mowings for six months before using as a mulch. Keep off garden plants.

BC 17 dicamba + MCPA + mecoprop

A mixture of three hormone weedkillers

see also under **Crop weedkillers** (AD)

Bio Weed Pencil   PBI   AL   04054

Control of broad-leaved weeds by spot treatment.

Invert bottle and squeeze gently to prime sponge pad. Apply by dabbing onto the centre and leaves of individual weeds. Re-treat as necessary.

BC 18 dicamba + MCPA + mecoprop with fertiliser

As former entry with addition of nitrogen (ammonium nitrate and urea) fertiliser

Fisons Lawncare Liquid   Fisons   SL   03625

Control of broad-leaved weeds and promotion of grass growth.

Apply with a watering can fitted with a fine rose or sprinkler bar on a calm, fine day between April and September when the soil is moist and the grass dry. Do not mow for 2–3 days after treatment. Repeat after six weeks if necessary. Do not use in drought or on lawns less than six months old.

Compost the first three mowings for at least six months before using on garden. Keep off garden plants.

BC 19 dichlorprop + ferrous sulphate + MCPA with fertiliser

A hormone weedkiller/mosskiller mixture combined with a nitrogen, phosphorus and potassium fertiliser

see also under **Lawn mosskillers** (BD)

J Arthur Bowers Feed & Weed
     + Mosskiller   Sinclair   GR   04188

Control of broad-leaved lawn weeds and moss and promotion of grass growth.

Apply at any time between late spring and early autumn. Do not mow for 2–3 days before or after application. Do not apply when grass wet or damp with dew but water thoroughly if it does not rain within 48 hours after application. Do not treat sown or laid lawns for the first year.

Do not use first four mowings after treatment for compost. Avoid contact with concrete or tarmac as staining may occur.

BC 20 dichlorprop + MCPA with fertiliser

A mixture of hormone weedkillers combined with a nitrogen, phosphorus and potassium fertiliser

1 Boots Lawn Feed & Weed Soluble Powder	Boots	SP	02403
2 Gateway Lawn Feed and Weedkiller	Sinclair	GR	04187
3 J Arthur Bowers Feed & Weed	Sinclair	GR	04186
4 Wilko Soluble Lawn Food and Weedkiller	Sinclair	SP	04391

Control of broad-leaved lawn weeds and promotion of grass growth.

Mix as directed and apply by watering can with a fine rose [1, 4], or apply granules by hand or with a spreader [2, 3], from late spring to early autumn, in warm weather when rain is not expected for a few

hours. Do not mow for four days before or after treatment [1], for 2−3 days before or after [2, 3], for three days after [4]. Repeat after eight weeks if necessary. Do not use in drought or on lawns less than six months old [1], one year old [2, 3]. Do not apply when grass wet or damp with dew but water thoroughly if it does not rain within 48 hours of application [2, 3].

Do not use mowings for mulch until composted for three months [1], six months [4], do not compost first four mowings [3].

BC 21 ferrous sulphate with fertiliser

A mosskiller based on an iron salt combined with sulphate of ammonia and other fertilisers which also has a scorching effect on lawn weeds

Numerous products

see entry under **Lawn mosskillers** (BD)

BC 22 glyphosate

A non-selective, non-residual, translocated weedkiller

see also under **Crop weedkillers** (AD), **Non-crop weedkillers** (EA)

Murphy Tumbleweed Gel   Fisons   PA   01457

Control of lawn weeds by spot treatment only.

Paint onto leaves of individual weeds with the brush provided, taking care to avoid all contact with lawn grasses. Apply when weeds making active growth, normally April to early November, and paint as large a weed leaf area as possible. Repeat if heavy rain falls within six hours. Re-sow any bare patches as soon as weeds are dead.

BC 23 MCPA + mecoprop with fertiliser

A mixture of hormone weedkillers combined with a nitrogen, phosphorus and potassium fertiliser

Fisons Evergreen 90   Fisons   GR   03131

Control of broad-leaved lawn weeds, including speedwell, and promotion of grass growth.

Apply evenly by hand or using a spreader between April and September in calm weather when the soil is moist and the grass dry. If no rain falls within 48 hours water thoroughly. Do not mow for 2−3 days before or after treatment. Repeat after six weeks if necessary. Do not use in drought or frosty weather or on lawns established for less than six months.

Do not use first three mowings after treatment for mulching until composted for six months. Keep off plants and tree foliage.

BC 24 **tar acids/tar oils** (cresylic acid)

Tar distillates used as general purpose sterilising agents which also have a scorching effect on lawn weeds

see also under **Crop chemicals** (AA, AC, AE), **Lawn mosskillers** (BD), **Greenhouse chemicals** (CD), **Non-crop mosskillers** (EB)

Murphy Mortegg   Fisons   EC 03616

Control of speedwell in lawns.

Apply in spring or summer when speedwell is growing actively under damp conditions, but not during rain. Grass is browned temporarily but recovers.

BD Lawn mosskillers

BD 1 **benazolin + 2, 4–D + dicamba + dichlorophen + dichlorprop + mecoprop with fertiliser**

A mixture of mosskiller and contact and hormone weedkillers combined with a nitrogen and potassium fertiliser

see also under **Lawn weedkillers** (BC), **Lawn wormkillers** (BE)

Boots Total Lawn Treatment   Boots   SL 00293

Control of moss, most lawn weeds and worms and promotion of grass growth.

Apply with a sprayer or watering can on a warm, still day between March and October. Moss control is best in June or July. Do not mow for four days before or after treatment. Do not apply in drought or when heavy rain or frost likely within four hours. Repeat treatment after twelve weeks if necessary.

Do not treat new lawns established for less than six months. Do not compost first mowing after treatment. Avoid drift of spray over garden plants and shrubs.

BD 2 **chloroxuron + dichlorophen + ferrous sulphate with fertiliser**

A mosskiller mixture combined with nitrogen fertiliser

Lawnsman Mosskiller   ICI   SP 03238

Control of moss and promotion of grass growth.

Apply with a sprayer or watering can in spring and repeat treatment in autumn if necessary. Do not apply under drought conditions or when frosty.

BD 3 **chloroxuron + ferric sulphate with fertiliser**

A mosskiller mixture combined with urea nitrogen fertiliser

Murphy Tumblemoss   Fisons   WP 03638

Control and prevention of moss on lawns.

Apply evenly with a watering can fitted with a fine rose between March and September; best results obtained in spring or autumn. The urea boosts the grass growth for two weeks, after which a suitable lawn fertiliser treatment is recommended. Further moss growth is prevented for up to twelve months.

BD 4 chloroxuron + ferrous sulphate

A mosskiller mixture

Ashlade D-Moss   Ashlade   GR   02831

A specially formulated lawn sand for moss control on lawns.

Apply when moss growing actively between spring and early autumn; best results obtained in late March/early April. Do not apply in drought, when frost imminent, if rain expected within 24 hours or within twelve months of sowing. Mow three days before application, water in if no rain falls within two days after application and do not walk on treated area until chemical has been washed in. Rake out dead moss after 4–6 weeks.

BD 5 2, 4–D + dicamba + ferrous sulphate with fertiliser

A hormone weedkiller/mosskiller mixture combined with a nitrogen, phosphorus and potassium fertiliser

see also under **Lawn weedkillers** (BC)

Triple Action Grasshopper   ICI   GR   03932

Control of moss and broad-leaved lawn weeds and promotion of grass growth.

Apply with special applicator provided, at any time during the growing season. Applicator may be re-used in conjunction with refill packs.

BD 6 2, 4–D + ferrous sulphate + mecoprop with fertiliser

A mosskiller/hormone weedkiller mixture combined with a nitrogen, phosphorus and potassium fertiliser

see also under **Lawn weedkillers** (BC)

1 ASDA Lawn Weed & Feed + Mosskiller	ASDA	GR	03819
2 Gem Lawn Weed & Feed + Mosskiller	Gem	GR	04488
3 Green-up Feed & Weed + Mosskiller	Synchemicals	GR	04450
4 M&B Supergreen Feed, Weed & Mosskiller	May & Baker	SP	03884
5 Vitax Weed'N'Feed Extra	Vitax	GR	03450

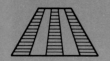

Control of moss and broad-leaved lawn weeds and promotion of grass growth.

Apply granules evenly on a still day in early spring and repeat in June or July [1-3, 5], when weeds growing actively between April and September using a watering can [4]. Apply 2-3 days before or after mowing [1, 2], mow three days before treatment and not again for at least four days after [3]. Water in if no rain falls for 48 hours; do not apply to wet grass or during drought; avoid walking on treated areas until chemical has been washed in [1-3, 5].

Do not use first three mowings as mulch until composted for six months. Do not use on sown or laid grass until established for at least twelve months.

BD 7   dichlorophen

A phenolic mosskiller, fungicide and algae killer

see also under **Lawn fungicides** (BB), **Greenhouse chemicals** (CD), **Non-crop mosskillers** (EB)

1 Bio Moss Killer	PBI	SL	00270
2 Fungo	Dax	SL	H1382
3 Moss Gun for Lawns and Paths	ICI	RH	03326

Control of moss on lawns and hard surfaces.

Apply with a sprayer or watering can [1, 2], as a ready-to-use spray [3], at any time of year; best results obtained in spring or early autumn. Repeat treatment after six weeks or as required. Do not apply in frost or drought. Avoid drift onto cultivated plants. Avoid contact with metal surfaces.

BD 8   dichlorophen with fertiliser

A mosskiller and fungicide combined with a nitrogen and phosphorus fertiliser

see also under **Lawn fungicides** (BB)

Boots Spring and Autumn Lawn Treatment	Boots	WP	03628

Control of moss and lawn diseases and promotion of grass growth.

Apply evenly with a watering can in spring or autumn. Do not mow for four days before or after treatment. Do not treat when frost or rain likely within four hours. Rake out dead moss after three weeks. Repeat treatment after twelve weeks if necessary.

BD 9   dichlorophen + ferrous sulphate with fertiliser

A mixture of mosskillers combined with a nitrogen fertiliser

1 Aitkens Lawn Sand Plus	Aitken	GR	04542
2 J Arthur Bowers Mosskiller	Sinclair	GR	04185

Control of moss on lawns and promotion of grass growth.

Apply evenly at any time between late spring and early autumn. Do not mow for 2–3 days before or after treatment. Do not apply when grass wet or damp with dew but water thoroughly if no rain falls for 48 hours. Rake out dead moss 7–10 days after application. Do not treat newly sown or laid lawns for first year. Avoid contact with concrete or tarmac as staining may occur.

BD 10 dichloroprop + ferrous sulphate + MCPA with fertiliser

A mosskiller/hormone weedkiller mixture combined with a nitrogen, phosphorus and potassium fertiliser

J Arthur Bowers Feed & Weed + Mosskiller	Sinclair	GR	04188

Control of moss and broad-leaved weeds on lawns.

See entry under **Lawn Weedkillers** (BC 19)

BD 11 ferrous sulphate

An iron salt with a contact action on moss and some weeds

Green-up Mossfree	Synchemicals	SP	03270

Fast-acting control of moss and lichens on lawns.

Mix as directed and apply with a sprayer or watering can in autumn or spring when the grass is moist and the moss growing actively. Best results obtained on a bright, still day when rain is not expected. Rake off dead moss after seven days. Repeat treatment after fourteen days if necessary.

BD 12 ferrous sulphate with fertiliser

As previous entry but combined with sulphate of ammonia to form lawn sand or with other fertilisers

1	ASDA Lawn Sand	ASDA	GR	04520
		(with sulphate of ammonia)		
2	Boots Lawn Moss Killer & Fertiliser	Boots	SP	02494
		(with nitrogen and potassium)		
3	Fisons Autumn Extra	Fisons	GR	03525
		(with nitrogen and potassium)		
4	Fisons Lawn Sand	Fisons	GR	00885
		(with sulphate of ammonia)		
5	Fisons Mosskil Extra	Fisons	GR	03267
		(with urea and sulphate of ammonia)		
6	Gateway Mosskiller with Fertiliser	Sinclair	GR	04224
		(with sulphate of ammonia)		

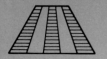

7	Gem Lawn Sand	Gem	GR	04555
		(with sulphate of ammonia)		
8	ICI Mosskiller for Lawns	ICI	GR	01389
		(with nitrogen, phosphorus and potassium)		
9	J Arthur Bowers Lawn Sand	Sinclair	GR	04083
		(with sulphate of ammonia)		
10	Maxicrop Mosskiller Lawn Tonic	Maxicrop	SL	02605
		(with seaweed extract)		
11	Mill Lawn Sand	Mill	GR	04536
		(with sulphate of ammonia)		
12	Notcutts Lawn Sand	Notcutt's	GR	04404
		(with sulphate of ammonia)		
13	PBI Velvas	PBI	GR	02291
		(with sulphate of ammonia)		
14	Vitax Lawn Sand	Vitax	GR	04352
		(with sulphate of ammonia)		
15	Wilko Lawn Sand	Sinclair	GR	04084
		(with sulphate of ammonia)		

Control of moss and some broad-leaved lawn weeds and promotion of grass growth.

Apply evenly when moss growing actively, usually in spring or autumn (in autumn only [3]), details of timing vary with product. Most products recommend mowing three days before treatment, not for 3–4 days after and raking up the dead moss after two weeks. One product [3] also recommended for use before sowing or turfing a new lawn. Do not treat in frosty weather or drought and water in if no rain falls for 48 hours after application. Avoid walking on lawn until chemical washed in.

Do not use on lawns established for less than twelve months [4, 13]. Keep off clothing, paving, etc., to avoid staining.

BD 13 **tar acids/tar oils** (cresylic acid)

Tar distillates used as general purpose sterilising agents

see also under **Crop chemicals** (AA, AC, AE), **Lawn weedkillers** (BC), **Greenhouse chemicals** (CD), **Non-crop mosskillers** (EB)

| 1 | Clean-Up | ICI | EC | 00539 |
| 2 | Murphy Mortegg | Fisons | EC | 03616 |

Control of moss, lichens, liverworts and algae on lawns and hard surfaces.

Apply with a sprayer or watering can when the moss is growing actively under damp conditions, but not during rain. Grass is browned but only temporarily.

BE Lawn wormkillers

BE 1 **benazolin + 2, 4–D + dicamba + dichlorophen + dichlorprop + mecoprop with fertiliser**

A mixture of weedkillers and mosskiller also active against worms combined with a nitrogen and potassium fertiliser

Boots Total Lawn Treatment   Boots   SL   00293

See entries under **Lawn weedkillers** (BC), **Lawn mosskillers** (BD)

BE 2 **carbaryl**

A carbamate wormkiller and insecticide

see also under **Crop chemicals** (AA), **Lawn insecticides** (BA), **Domestic insecticides** (GA)

Murphy Lawn Pest Killer   Fisons   SC   04433

Controls worms and insect pests on lawns.

Apply with a sprayer or watering can in April and/or September or when pests active. Control lasts for up to six months. Mow before treatment; after treatment, if mowing is needed before a good rain has fallen, mow without grass box. Later mowings may be composted.

BE 3 **carbaryl with fertiliser**

A carbamate wormkiller and insecticide combined with a high phosphate, low nitrogen fertiliser

see also under **Lawn insecticides** (BA)

PBI Autumn & Winter Toplawn   PBI   GR   00172

Control of worms and leatherjackets combined with root feeding of grass.

Apply evenly by hand or with a lawn spreader between September and April or when preparing to sow or turf new lawn.

BE 4 **(chlordane)**

A persistent organochlorine wormkiller and insecticide, approvals for home garden use of which were revoked at the end of 1988. It is no longer legal for garden centres or other suppliers to stock this chemical for sale to amateur gardeners. It is also illegal for amateur gardeners to store or use chlordane. Any gardeners with remaining stocks of this chemical should consult the local authority waste disposal department for advice on disposal.

C Greenhouse Chemicals

CA Greenhouse insecticides
CA 1   bioallethrin + permethrin
CA 2   bromophos
CA 3   dichlorvos
CA 4   dichlorvos + gamma-HCH + tetramethrin
CA 5   dimethoate + permethrin
CA 6   fatty acids
CA 7   heptenophos + permethrin
CA 8   malathion
CA 9   permethrin
CA 10   pirimicarb
CA 11   pirimiphos-methyl
CA 12   pirimiphos-methyl + pyrethrins
CA 13   pyrethrins/pyrethrum
CA 14   pyrethrins/pyrethrum + resmethrin
CA 15   quassia + rotenone (derris)
CA 16   rotenone (derris)

CB Greenhouse fungicides
CB 1   benomyl
CB 2   carbendazim
CB 3   copper oxychloride
CB 4   copper sulphate
CB 5   mancozeb
CB 6   thiophanate-methyl

CC Greenhouse fungicide/insecticide mixtures
CC 1   dimethoate + gamma-HCH + thiram
CC 2   gamma-HCH + tecnazene
CC 3   rotenone (derris) + sulphur

CD Greenhouse disinfectants
CD 1   dichlorophen
CD 2   quaternary ammonium compounds
CD 3   sulphur
CD 4   tar acids/tar oils (cresylic acid)

CA Greenhouse insecticides

CA 1   **bioallethrin + permethrin**
A mixture of fast acting, contact pyrethroid insecticides
see also under **House plant chemicals** (D), **Domestic insecticides** (GA, GB)
Boots Kill-A-Bug Spray Gun   Boots   RH   03957
See entry under **Crop insecticides** (AA 2)

CA 2 **bromophos**

A contact and stomach-acting organophosphorus insecticide

PBI Bromophos   PBI   GR   00340

See entry under **Crop insecticides** (AA 5)

CA 3 **dichlorvos**

A contact and stomach-acting organophosphorus insecticide

see also under **Domestic insecticides** (GB)

1 Sectovap Greenhouse Pest
   Killer   Secto   VP   03650
2 Vapona Fly Killer   Nicholas   VP   H1645

Control of greenfly, blackfly, whitefly, red spider mite, leaf miners and many other pests on greenhouse plants, including tomatoes.

Suspend the unit in the greenhouse as directed. Protection is provided for up to four months. Do not use on tomatoes or cucumbers before the first flowers appear. Do not use on chrysanthemum varieties *Dawn Star* and *Hurricane* or on any Taffetas or Shastas.

CA 4 **dichlorvos + gamma-HCH + tetramethrin**

An insecticide mixture combining contact, ingested, fumigant and fast knock-down activity

Secto Aphid Killer   Secto   AE   03704

See entry under **Crop insecticides** (AA 9)

CA 5 **dimethoate + permethrin**

An insecticide mixture combining systemic, contact and residual activity

1 Bio Longlast   PBI   EC   00269
2 Secto Systemic Insect Killer
   Concentrate   Secto   LI   02950

See entry under **Crop insecticides** (AA 11)

CA 6 **fatty acids**

A contact-acting, soap concentrate insecticide

1 Safers Fruit & Vegetable
   Insecticide   Phostrogen   RH   04329
2 Safers Rose & Flower
   Insecticide   Phostrogen   RH   04341
3 Savona   Koppert   SL   03137

See entry under **Crop insecticides** (AA 12)

CA 7   heptenophos + permethrin

A mixture of a systemic organophosphorus and a contact-acting pyrethroid insecticide

Murphy Tumblebug	Fisons	RH	03637

See entry under **Crop insecticides** (AA 17)

CA 8   malathion

A contact-acting organophosphorus insecticide and acaricide

1	Green Fly Aerosol Spray	B.H. & B.	AE	01002
2	Malathion Dust	B.H. & B.	DP	01241
3	Malathion 50 Liquid Spray	B.H. & B.	LI	01249
4	Murphy Liquid Malathion	Fisons	LI	01248
5	Murphy Malathion Dust	Fisons	DP	01244
6	PBI Malathion Greenfly Killer	PBI	LI	01247

See entry under **Crop insecticides** (AA 18)

CA 9   permethrin

A contact acting pyrethroid insecticide with good residual activity

see also under **Crop insecticides** (AA), **House plant chemicals** (D), **Domestic insecticides** (GA)

1	Bio Sprayday	PBI	EC	00272
2	Boots Caterpillar and Whitefly Killer	Boots	EC	00290
3	Fumite Whitefly Cones	ICI	FU	00946
4	Murphy Permethrin Whitefly Smokes	Fisons	FU	01459
5	Picket	ICI	EC	01590

Control of whitefly, caterpillars and thrips on all common edible and ornamental greenhouse plants [3, 4].
See entry under **Crop insecticides** (AA 20) [1, 2, 5].

Fumigate in late afternoon or evening as soon as pests appear and repeat as necessary, for whitefly every 7–10 days. Light cones after closing all vents and keep the greenhouse closed for at least four hours, preferably overnight. Ensure that plant roots are moist and the foliage dry. Avoid spraying delicate open blooms [1]. Slight scorch may occur on pot geraniums, begonias, vines, ferns and succulents [2]. Do not treat roses, schizanthus, orchids or tender young seedlings [3]. Do not fumigate rare or unusual plants without first testing on a small scale [4].

Ventilate greenhouse for one hour before re-entry. Do not breathe smoke. Extremely dangerous to fish. Food crops can be picked as soon as fumigation is complete.

CA 10 pirimicarb

A fast-acting, selective and non-persistent carbamate aphid killer

1 Rapid	ICI	EC	01690
2 Rapid Aerosol	ICI	AE	01689

See entry under **Crop insecticides** (AA 22)

CA 11 pirimiphos-methyl

A fast-acting organophosphorus insecticide and acaricide with contact and fumigant action

see also under **Crop insecticides** (AA), **Lawn insecticides** (BA)

1 Fumite General Purpose Insecticide Smoke Cones	ICI	FU	00932
2 ICI Antkiller	ICI	DP	00101
3 Sybol	ICI	EC	02058

Control of whitefly, red spider mite, greenfly, leaf miners, leafhoppers, mealybug, thrips, fungus gnats, woodlice and ants on all common greenhouse plants [1].
See entry under **Crop insecticides** (AA 23) [2, 3].

Fumigate in late afternoon or evening as soon as pests appear and repeat as necessary, for whitefly every 3–4 days, for red spider mite every seven days. Light cones after closing all vents and keep greenhouse closed for at least four hours, preferably overnight. Ensure that plant roots are moist and the foliage dry. Do not fumigate rare or unusual plants without first testing on a small scale. Do not treat roses, schizanthus, orchids or tender young seedlings.

Ventilate greenhouse for one hour before re-entry. Do not breathe smoke. Extremely dangerous to fish. Food crops can be picked as soon as fumigation is complete.

CA 12 pirimiphos-methyl + pyrethrins

As previous entry with addition of pyrethrins and formulation as an aerosol

Sybol Aerosol	ICI	AE	03597

See entry under **Crop insecticides** (AA 24)

CA 13 pyrethrins/pyrethrum

Non-persistent, contact insecticides of natural origin based on extracts of pyrethrum flowers

1 Bio Friendly Anti-Ant Duster	PBI	DP	00098
2 Bug Gun for Fruit and Vegetables	ICI	RH	03076

3	Bug Gun for Roses and Flowers	ICI	RH	03076
4	Gateway Pest Spray for Fruit and Vegetables	Sinclair	RH	03985
5	Gateway Pest Spray for Roses and Flowers	Sinclair	RH	03986
6	Py Garden Insecticide	Synchemicals	AE	02811
7	Py Powder	Synchemicals	DP	02809
8	Py Spray Garden Insect Killer	Synchemicals	LI	02810

See entry under **Crop insecticides** (AA 25).

CA 14   pyrethrins/pyrethrum + resmethrin

As previous entry with addition of a powerful non-persistent contact-acting pyrethroid insecticide

1	Doom Garden Insect Killer Aerosol	Napa Products	AE	00747
2	Doom Greenhouse & Garden Insect Killer	Napa Products	AE	02694
3	Rentokil Blackfly & Greenfly Killer	Rentokil	AE	02984
4	Rentokil Greenhouse & Garden Insect Killer	Rentokil	AE	02983

See entry under **Crop insecticides** (AA 26).

CA 15   quassia + rotenone (derris)

A mixture of insecticides of natural origin

| Bio Friendly Insect Spray | PBI | SL | 00180 |

See entry under **Crop insecticides** (AA 28)

CA 16   rotenone (derris)

A natural insecticide of short persistence extracted from roots of Derris and related plants

1	Derris Dust	B.H. & B.	DP	00672
2	Derris Dust (ex Corry's Derris Dust)	Synchemicals	DP	00676
3	Doff Derris Dust	Doff	DP	00740
4	ICI Derris Dust (ex Abol Derris Dust)	ICI	DP	02651
5	Murphy Derris Dust	Fisons	DP	00674
6	PBI Liquid Derris	PBI	EC	01214

See entry under **Crop insecticides** (AA 29).

CB Greenhouse fungicides

CB 1 benomyl
A broad-spectrum, protective and curative systemic fungicide
see also under **Lawn fungicides (BB)**, **House plant chemicals (D)**

Benlate + Activex	ICI	WP	02491

See entry under **Crop fungicides (AB 1)**.

CB 2 carbendazim
A broad-spectrum, protective and curative systemic fungicide
see also under **Crop fungicides (AB)**, **Lawn fungicides (BB)**

PBI Supercarb	PBI	WP	03891

Control of powdery mildew, grey mould, stem rot, bulb and corm rots and other diseases of greenhouse plants.

Apply as a protective spray or when disease first appears. Bulbs and corms may be dipped or dusted before planting. Do not spray plants suffering from drought or during hot conditions.

CB 3 copper oxychloride
A general purpose, protective copper-based fungicide

Murphy Traditional Copper Fungicide	Fisons	WP	04585

Control of damping off and footrot of seedlings.
See entry under **Crop fungicides (AB 4)**.

CB 4 copper sulphate
(a) copper sulphate + ammonium carbonate
A mixture protecting seedlings against damping off

1 Cheshunt Compound	B.H. & B.	SP	00484
2 PBI Cheshunt Compound	PBI	SP	00485

(b) copper sulphate + ammonium hydroxide
A general purpose, ready-to-use fungicide mixture

Spraydex General Purpose Fungicide	Spraydex	RH	02865

(c) copper sulphate + calcium hydroxide (Bordeaux Mixture)
A mixture controlling blight and many other fungus diseases

1 Bordeaux Mixture	B.H. & B.	SP	00296
2 Bordeaux Mixture	Synchemicals	SP	00297

See **copper sulphate mixtures** under **Crop fungicides (AB 5)**.

CB 5　mancozeb

A protective fungicide for control of blight and many other diseases, also containing zinc and manganese trace elements

Dithane 945　　　　　　　　　PBI　　　　　　　WP　00718

See entry under **Crop fungicides** (AB 6).

CB 6　thiophanate-methyl

A broad-spectrum protective and curative systemic fungicide

see also under **Lawn fungicides** (BB)

M & B Systemic Fungicide Liquid　May & Baker　　SC　00952

See entry under **Crop fungicides** (AB 12).

CC　Greenhouse fungicide/insecticide mixtures

CC 1　dimethoate + gamma-HCH + thiram

A mixture of systemic and contact insecticides and acaricides with a protective fungicide

see also under **House plant chemicals** (D)

1　Secto Garden Powder　　　Secto　　　　　DP　02774
2　Secto Rose and Flower Spray　Secto　　　　　RH　03843

See entry under **Crop fungicide/insecticide mixtures** (AC 4).

CC 2　gamma-HCH + tecnazene

Dual purpose insecticide/fungicide mixtures formulated as fumigant smokes

1　Fumite Tecnalin Smoke Cones　ICI　　　　　FU　00944
2　Murphy Pest and Disease
　　Smokes　　　　　　　　　Fisons　　　　　FU　03973

Control of botrytis (grey mould) and insect pests (including greenfly, whitefly, capsid bugs, leaf miners, thrips, earwigs, ants, etc.) on greenhouse tomatoes, lettuce, chrysanthemums and other ornamentals.

Apply in late afternoon or early evening, not in bright sunshine or windy weather. Light cones after closing all vents and keep greenhouse closed overnight. For botrytis control on tomatoes fumigate every three weeks from third truss stage. Ensure that plant roots are moist and the foliage dry before fumigating. Do not use on cucumbers, melons, roses, schizanthus, orchids, hydrangeas or young seedlings.

Do not breathe smoke. Ventilate greenhouse for one hour before re-entry. Do not pick food crops within two days of treatment. Remove domestic animals and birds from vicinity of greenhouse during treatment.

CC 3 **rotenone** (derris) **+ sulphur**

A mixture of natural insecticide and fungicide

Bio Friendly Pest & Disease
Duster PBI DP 00265

See entry under **Crop fungicide/insecticide mixtures** (AC 7).

CD Greenhouse disinfectants

CD 1 **dichlorophen**

A phenolic fungicide and algae, moss and lichen killer

see also under **Lawn chemicals** (BB, BC), **Non-crop mosskillers** (EB)

1 Algofen	Geeco	SL	02392
2 Fungo	Dax	SL	H1382

Disinfection of greenhouse structures, staging, seed trays, pots, etc.

Dilute as directed and spray, dip, wipe or brush on surfaces as appropriate.

CD 2 **quaternary ammonium compounds**

A concentrated disinfectant for house and garden use

Garden Jack House & Garden
Disinfectant PBI SL *

* not classed as a pesticide.

Disinfection and cleaning of seed trays, pots, greenhouse staging, etc. May also be used in and around home.

Use as recommended.

CD 3 **sulphur**

A combustible chemical formulated for use as a fumigant

see also under **Crop fungicides** (AB)

Sulphur Candles B.H. & B. FU 02039

Fumigation of greenhouses and other spaces.

Light candles after removing all plants, except dormant peaches and vines, and ensuring that all doors, windows, etc., are closed. Leave for twelve hours before opening up house and ventilating.

Do not breathe gas. Prevent access during fumigation until after the area has been well ventilated.

CD 4   **tar acids/tar oils** (cresylic acid)

Tar distillates used as general purpose sterilising agents

see also under **Crop chemicals** (AA, AC, AE), **Lawn chemicals** (BC, BD), **Non-crop mosskillers** (EB)

1 Armillatox	Armillatox	EC	00115
2 Clean-Up	ICI	EC	00539
3 Jeyes Fluid	Jeyes	EC	04606

Disinfection of greenhouse structures, staging, seed trays, pots, etc. and sterilisation of soil.

Dilute as directed and spray or otherwise apply to interior structures in late autumn, ideally twice a year. Apply as a drench in autumn for soil sterilisation.

D House Plant Chemicals

D 1   benomyl

A broad-spectrum protective and curative systemic fungicide

see also under **Lawn fungicides** (BB), **Greenhouse fungicides** (CB)

Benlate + Activex   ICI   WP 02491

See entry under **Crop fungicides** (AB 1).

D 2   bioallethrin + permethrin

A pyrethroid insecticide mixture with fast knock-down and residual activity

see also under **Crop insecticides** (AA), **Greenhouse insecticides** (CA), **Domestic insecticides** (GA, GB)

Spraydex Houseplant Spray   Spraydex   RH H3450

Control of greenfly, blackfly, whitefly, midges, red spider mite, caterpillars, thrips, mealybug and other insect pests on house plants, and of many crawling insects around the home.

Spray at first signs of pest attack and repeat as necessary.

D 3   butoxycarboxim

A systemic aphicide and acaricide

Plant Pins   Phostrogen   IM 01599

Prevention and control of greenfly, thrips, red spider mite, and other mites on house plants. May also be used in outdoor planters and pot plants in the greenhouse.

Insert 'pins' into growing medium so that they are completely buried and water normally. Do not use on abutilon, calceolaria, Christmas pepper, cineraria, cordyline, maidenhair fern, nasturtium, poinsettia, primrose, winter cherry or any edible plants. Treatment becomes effective after 2–7 days.

D 4 **dimethoate with fertiliser**

A systemic insecticide and acaricide combined with a controlled release fertiliser

see also under **Crop insecticides** (AA)

Keriguards ICI TB 03299

Protection against greenfly, mealybug, red spider mite and other pests and provision of plant food for pot plants and hanging baskets.

Press tablets into growing medium until completely covered, water well and allow to drain, thereafter water normally. Use every two months when plants are growing. Do not use on adiantum, chrysanthemum, hibiscus, saintpaulia or young, recently potted plants.

D 5 **dimethoate + gamma-HCH + thiram**

A mixture of systemic and contact-acting insecticides combined with a protective fungicide

see also under **Crop chemicals** (AC), **Greenhouse chemicals** (CC)

Secto Flora Spray Systemic
    Insect Killer Secto RH 03843

Control of insect pests (including greenfly, blackfly, whitefly, red spider mite) and diseases (including downy mildew, blight, etc.) on house plants.

Apply ready-to-use spray when pest or disease first appears and repeat treatment as necessary.

D 6 **fatty acids**

A contact-acting, soap concentrate insecticide

see also under **Crop insecticides** (AA), **Greenhouse insecticides** (CA)

Safer's House Plant Insecticide Phostrogen RH 04328

Control of whitefly, greenfly, mealybug, red spider mite, scale insects, thrips, etc. on house plants.

Spray thoroughly at first signs of attack and repeat as necessary. Do not spray ferns.

D 7   **permethrin**

A contact-acting pyrethroid insecticide with good residual activity

see also under **Crop insecticides** (AA), **Greenhouse insecticides** (CA), **Domestic insecticides** (GA)

1	Bio Flydown	PBI	EC 00267
2	Bio Sprayday	PBI	EC 00272
3	Fisons Insect Spray for Houseplants	Fisons	AE 02521

Control of greenfly, whitefly, red spider mite, mealybug, scale insects, caterpillars and other insect pests on house plants [1, 3], and of household pests [1].
See entry under **Crop insecticides** (AA 20).

Spray at first signs of pest attack and repeat as necessary, every four days for whitefly. Do not spray open blooms, nor in hot sunshine.

Dangerous to bees. Extremely dangerous to fish.

D 8   **pirimiphos-methyl + pyrethrins**

A combination of a fast-acting organophosphorus insecticide with pyrethrins

see also under **Crop insecticides** (AA), **Greenhouse insecticides** (CA), **Domestic insecticides** (GA, GB)

Kerispray	ICI	AE 02653

Control of whitefly, red spider mite, greenfly, mealybug, scale insects, fungus gnats and other insect pests of house plants.

Spray at first signs of pest attack and repeat as necessary, for whitefly every four days, for red spider mite every seven days. Do not use on cacti, ferns or succulents. Do not spray open blooms.

D 9   **pyrazophos**

A systemic fungicide active against mildew

see also under **Crop fungicides** (AB)

Pokon Mildew Spray	Chrysal	AE 01610

Prevention and control of mildew on begonias, geraniums, saintpaulias and other house plants and on garden perennials, roses and other shrubs.

Spray gently from about 30 cm (12 in) away as soon as infection visible and repeat after ten days if necessary. Hold can in inverted position to spray underside of leaves. Spraying open blooms may cause damage to house plants.

Dangerous to bees; do not spray open flowers.

D 10 pyrethrins/pyrethrum + resmethrin

A mixture of pyrethrins with a powerful, non-persistent contact-acting pyrethroid insecticide

see also under **Crop insecticides** (AA), **Greenhouse insecticides** (CA)

1 Rentokil Houseplant Insect Killer	Rentokil	AE	02985
2 Synchemicals House Plant Pest Killer	Synchemicals	AE	02734

Control of greenfly, blackfly, whitefly, red spider mite and many other insect pests of house plants.

Spray at first signs of pest attack and repeat as necessary, for whitefly and red spider mite at 4–5 day intervals. Do not spray open blooms.

E Non-crop Weed and Moss Killers

EA Non-crop weedkillers

EA 1	aminotriazole (amitrole) + atrazine
EA 2	aminotriazole (amitrole) + atrazine + 2, 4–D
EA 3	aminotriazole (amitrole) + 2, 4–D + diuron + simazine
EA 4	aminotriazole (amitrole) + diquat + paraquat + simazine
EA 5	aminotriazole (amitrole) + MCPA
EA 6	aminotriazole (amitrole) + MCPA + simazine
EA 7	aminotriazole (amitrole) + simazine
EA 8	ammonium sulphamate
EA 9	atrazine + sodium chlorate
EA 10	2, 4–D + dicamba + mecoprop
EA 11	dalapon
EA 12	dicamba + dichlorprop + MCPA
EA 13	dichlobenil
EA 14	diquat + paraquat
EA 15	diuron + simazine
EA 16	glyphosate
EA 17	simazine
EA 18	sodium chlorate

EB Non-crop mosskillers

EB 1	carbendazim + quaternary ammonium compounds
EB 2	dichlorophen
EB 3	tar acids/tar oils (cresylic acid)

EC Products for algae control in ponds

EC 1	tannic acid

EA Non-crop weedkillers

EA 1 aminotriazole (amitrole) + atrazine

A non-selective mixture of a translocated and a residual weedkiller

1 Boots Long-Lasting Weedkiller	Boots	WP	03806
2 Dee Weed	Arable & Bulb	SC	00659
3 FS Total Weedkiller	Ford Smith	WP	04167
4 Murphy Path Weed Killer	Fisons	SC	03630

Control of existing weeds, including docks, dandelions, grasses and most other annual and perennial weeds on paths and drives.

Apply when weeds growing actively (best between April and August), when rain not expected for four hours. Regrowth is prevented for 6–12 months (longer at higher rates). Do not use under trees or shrubs or on land intended for cropping. Do not apply on slopes where run-off may wash chemical onto lawns or beds.

EA 2 aminotriazole (amitrole) + atrazine + 2, 4–D

As previous entry with addition of a hormone weedkiller

Rentokil Path & Patio Weedkiller   Rentokil   AE   02873

Control of all types of weed on paths, patios and other hard surfaces.

Spray weed foliage until covered with foam. May be used between April and October. Regrowth is prevented for up to two years.

EA 3 aminotriazole (amitrole) + 2, 4–D + diuron + simazine

A non-selective mixture of two translocated and two residual weedkillers

Hytrol   Agrichem   WP   04540

Control of all types of weed on paths, drives and other situations where no vegetation is wanted.

May be used at any time of year but best between April and September when weed growth is rapid. Rain shortly after spraying does not reduce efficacy. Regrowth is prevented for up to two years. Avoid spray drift onto lawns or plants. Do not apply on slopes where run-off may wash chemical onto lawns or beds.

EA 4 aminotriazole (amitrole) + diquat + paraquat + simazine

A non-selective mixture of one translocated, two fast-acting contact and a residual weedkiller

Pathclear   ICI   SG   01546

Control of all types of weed on paths, drives and waste ground.

Dissolve granules as directed and apply at any time of year with a special applicator or a watering can fitted with a sprinkler bar or fine rose. Light rain shortly after treatment does not reduce efficacy. Do not use on lawns, flower beds or other cultivated areas. Do not apply on slopes where run-off may wash chemical onto lawns or beds.

EA 5 aminotriazole (amitrole) + MCPA

A non-selective mixture of two translocated weedkillers

1 Fisons Problem Weeds Killer   Fisons   SL   02871
2 Murphy Problem Weeds Killer   Fisons   SL   04320

Control of nettles, thistles, bindweed, docks, knotgrass, plantains, horsetail, briars, brambles and other weeds on uncultivated ground and as a spot treatment amongst trees and shrubs.

Apply with a watering can fitted with a fine rose or sprinkler bar on a calm, dry day between April and September when the weeds are growing strongly. For spot treatment apply with a 'squeezy' bottle, but take care to keep off cultivated plants. Well established perennial weeds may need more than one application. Do not plant treated areas for three months after treatment.

EA 6 aminotriazole (amitrole) + MCPA + simazine

A non-selective mixture of two translocated and a residual weedkiller

Fisons Path Weeds Killer	Fisons	SC	02700

Control of all types of weed on paths and drives for a full season.

Apply using a watering can fitted with a fine rose at any time of year, best in early spring. Do not use on lawns, flower beds or vegetables and avoid drift. Do not apply beneath shallow rooted shrubs or trees or underneath stone fruit.

EA 7 aminotriazole (amitrole) + simazine

A non-selective mixture of a translocated and a residual weedkiller

1	M&B Path & Drive Weedkiller	May & Baker	SC	02738
2	Murphy Super Weedex	Fisons	SC	02054

Control of all types of weed on paths, drives, patios and other hard surfaces for a full season.

Apply using a watering can fitted with a fine rose or sprinkler bar between April and September when the weeds are in active growth. Regrowth is prevented for up to twelve months. Do not disturb soil after application. Do not use under trees or shrubs or on land intended for planting. Do not apply on slopes where run-off may wash chemical onto flower beds or lawns.

EA 8 ammonium sulphamate

A crystalline salt used as a non-selective weedkiller

1	Amcide	B.H. & B.	CR	00089
2	Root-Out	Dax	CR	03510

See entry under **Crop weedkillers** (AD 2).

EA 9 atrazine + sodium chlorate (with fire depressant)

A non-selective mixture of sodium chlorate with a residual weedkiller

Atlacide Extra Dusting Powder	Chipman	DP	00124

Control of all types of weed on paths, drives, etc.

Sprinkle dust evenly over foliage, using a shaker tin, at any time of year during the growing season; best in spring or early summer. Do not apply before heavy rain.

Clothing, paper, timber and plant debris become highly inflammable if contaminated with sodium chlorate. If clothes become contaminated wash them thoroughly and do not stand near an open fire.

EA 10   2, 4–D + dicamba + mecoprop

A mixture of translocated weedkillers for control of perennial weeds

New Formula SBK Brushwood
        Killer   Synchemicals   EC   02941

Control of nettles, thistles, brambles, briars, bindweed, docks and many other perennial and woody weeds.

For perennial weeds, mix with water and spray in March–July, when weeds in active growth. For brambles, briars and saplings, mix with paraffin and spray in June–September. Mix with oil to treat stumps and sucker regrowth. See label for details.

Do not allow spray to drift onto fruit, flowers or vegetables; do not use in hot or windy conditions. Keep animals out of areas being treated; do not cut or graze for at least seven days. Keep livestock out of treated areas until foliage of any poisonous weeds, such as ragwort, has died and become unpalatable. Do not cultivate or replant land for at least six weeks after treatment.

EA 11   dalapon

A translocated weedkiller active against grass weeds

see also under **Crop weedkillers** (AD)

Synchemicals Couch & Grass
        Killer   Synchemicals   SP   02735

Control of couch, creeping bent, Yorkshire fog, creeping soft grass and other annual and perennial grass weeds in uncultivated land and certain crops.

Spray from March to October when grass weeds are growing strongly. Normal cultivation may commence 6–8 weeks after treatment, seed sowing or replanting twelve weeks after spraying. Chemical can be mixed with New Formula SBK Brushwood Killer to give combined kill of grasses and broad-leaved weeds. Do not apply in frost or drought. Rain within twelve hours of spraying will reduce effectiveness.

EA 12   dicamba + dichlorprop + MCPA

A mixture of translocated weedkillers for perennial and woody weed control

see also under **Lawn weedkillers** (BC)

Boots Nettle & Bramble
        Weedkiller   Boots   SL   03455

Control of nettles, docks, thistles, ground elder, brambles and briars in rough grass and hedge bottoms; reduction in regrowth from tree stumps.

Apply to foliage, using a watering can with a fine rose, on a warm day when weeds are in full leaf between May and September. Repeat after eight weeks if necessary. If using under hedges, direct spray at base of hedge and do not use under hedges less than two years old. For stump treatment drill holes in stump and apply with a stiff brush.

Avoid spray drift onto garden plants.

EA 13 dichlobenil

A residual, soil-acting weedkiller with selective and non-selective uses

see also under **Crop weedkillers** (AD)

Casoron G4   Synchemicals   GR   00450

Control of all types of annual and some perennial weeds, including docks, nettles, field horsetail, creeping thistle, rosebay willowherb, ground elder and couch, and prevention of regrowth on paths, drives, hard tennis courts, etc.

Apply evenly from March to early May, avoiding settled spells of warm weather. Weed growth is controlled for up to twelve months. Chemical does not creep sideways and can be applied up to the edges of lawns and borders, provided that no granules fall on them.

Do not apply in or near greenhouses. Store well away from bulbs, corms, tubers and seeds.

EA 14 diquat + paraquat

A non-selective, non-persistent, general purpose contact weedkiller

see also under **Crop weedkillers** (AD)

Weedol   ICI   SG   01491

Control of annual weeds, grasses and top growth of perennials on paths, drives, uncultivated land and between garden plants. Also for clearing ground prior to cultivation.

Dissolve granules as directed and apply with ICI Applicator or a watering can fitted with a sprinkler bar or fine rose. May be used up to the base of trees and shrubs but ensure that liquid does not come into contact with cultivated plants or lawn grasses. Chemical is inactivated on contact with soil. Rain falling after treatment does not reduce efficacy.

EA 15 diuron + simazine

A non-selective mixture of residual weedkillers

M&B Total Weedkiller Granules   May & Baker   GR   03259

Control of all types of weed and preventinn of regrowth on paths, patios and other hard surfaces.

Sprinkle granules on areas to be treated. Treatment provides season-long control.

EA 16 glyphosate

A non-selective, non-residual translocated weedkiller

see also under **Crop weedkillers** (AD), **Lawn weedkillers** (BC)

1 Greenscape Weedkiller	Monsanto	SL	04321
2 Murphy Ready-to-Use Tumbleweed Sprayer	Fisons	RH	01458
3 Murphy Tumbleweed	Fisons	SL	01456
4 Murphy Tumbleweed Gel	Fisons	PA	01457

Control of most types of annual and perennial weeds and grasses, including couch, creeping thistle and docks, on paths, drives, uncultivated land and between garden plants.

Apply as a light spray [2], by sprayer or watering can with a fine rose or sprinkler bar [1, 3], with the brush provided [4], on a dry day from spring to autumn. Repeat if heavy rain falls within six hours. Treat nettles and ground elder in late spring, if treating later in the season, cut to ground level and spray the regrowth. Treat horsetail from early July. Other perennials may also need re-treatment. Do not use galvanised or mild steel watering cans or sprayers. Avoid all contact with cultivated plants or lawn grass. Crops can be planted the day after treating a light cover of annual weeds; allow seven days after treating a dense cover which includes perennials.

EA 17 simazine

A persistent residual soil-acting weedkiller

see also under **Crop weedkillers** (AD)

Murphy Weedex   Fisons   WP   02352

Control of all types of weed on paths, drives and patios.

Apply using a watering can with a fine rose or sprinkler bar between April and September. The chemical acts via the soil rather than the leaves and has little effect on established weeds but new weed establishment is prevented for up to twelve months. Do not use at the total weed control rate under trees or shrubs or on land intended for planting. Do not apply on slopes where run-off may wash the chemical onto lawns or beds.

EA 18 sodium chlorate (with fire depressant)

A non-selective mineral salt weedkiller (also a strong oxidising agent and therefore formulated with a fire depressant)

1 Cookes Liquid Sodium Chlorate Weedkiller	Cooke	SL	04280
2 Cookes Sodium Chlorate Weedkiller	Cooke	SP	04281
3 Doff Sodium Chlorate	Doff	SP	00500
4 Gem Sodium Chlorate	Gem	SP	04276
5 ICI Sodium Chlorate	ICI	SP	01973
6 Lever Sodium Chlorate	Lever	SP	02819
7 Murphy Sodium Chlorate	Fisons	SP	03635
8 Sodium Chlorate	B.H. & B.	SP	01972
9 Sodium Chlorate (Fire Suppressed) Weedkiller	Ace	SP	04445

Control of annual and many perennial broad-leaved weeds and grasses on paths, drives, courtyards, hard tennis courts and waste land. May also be used to kill tree stumps [5].

Apply solution using a watering can with a fine rose. Best results obtained when applied in damp weather but do not apply if heavy rain expected. Residual effects last for at least six months. Keep well away from lawns, flowers and trees or shrubs with spreading roots. Do not apply on sloping ground where chemical may be washed onto lawns and beds. Do not plant on treated ground for at least six months or, in the case of beetroot, swedes or turnips, for twelve months. To kill tree stumps drill holes in cut surface, fill with powder and top up with water, adding further chemical as necessary [5].

Clothing, paper, wood and other organic materials become highly inflammable if contaminated. Keep off clothing. Not to be sold to persons under 18. Harmful if swallowed and in contact with skin or eyes.

EB Non-crop mosskillers

EB 1 carbendazim + quaternary ammonium compounds

A combined fungicide, mosskiller and algae killer

Rentokil Exterior Mouldicide Trispot	Rentokil	LI	H2111

Control and prevention of mould, algae, moss and lichen on hard surfaces outside the home.

Use straight from bottle. Product is formulated with resin for application to glass, metal, wood, brickwork and masonry and gives protection for up to twelve months. Does not stain or discolour surfaces.

EB 2 dichlorophen

A phenolic fungicide, mosskiller and algae killer

see also under **Lawn chemicals** (BB, BD), **Greenhouse chemicals** (CD)

1 Bio Moss Killer	PBI	SL	00270
2 Fungo	Dax	SL	H1382
3 Moss Gun for Lawns and Paths	ICI	RH	03326

Control of moss, lichen and algae on paths, drives, patios, walls and other hard surfaces and on lawns.

Dilute as directed and apply with sprayer or watering can [1, 2], apply as ready-to-use spray [3], at any time of year (best in spring and/or early autumn). Repeat treatment after six weeks or as required. Do not apply in frost or drought. Avoid drift onto cultivated plants. Avoid contact with metal surfaces.

EB 3 tar acids/tar oils (cresylic acid)

Tar distillates used as general purpose sterilising agents

see also under **Crop chemicals** (AA, AC, AE), **Lawn chemicals** (BC), **Greenhouse chemicals** (CD)

1 Clean-Up	ICI	EC	00539
2 Murphy Mortegg	Fisons	EC	03616

See entry under **Lawn mosskillers** (BD 13).

EC Products for algae control in ponds

EC 1 tannic acid

A flocculating agent causing settling out of suspended matter

Green-Away for Ponds	Interpet	SL	*

* product not subject to Pesticides legislation.

Clears green and cloudy water in ponds and aquaria.

Add required amount of product to bucket of pond water, mix well and disperse throughout pond. Siphon or filter out sediment within five hours of treatment.

General Chemicals

F   Slug and snail killers

F 1   aluminium sulphate
F 2   aluminium sulphate + copper sulphate + potassium permanganate
F 3   copper sulphate + ferrous sulphate
F 4   metaldehyde
F 5   methiocarb

F 1   aluminium sulphate

A metallic salt killing slugs and snails by contact action

1 Fertosan Slug & Snail Killer	Fertosan	SP	00864
2 Growing Success Slug Killer	Growing Success	SP	04386
3 Septico Slug Killer	Septico	SG	02562
4 6x Slug Killer	Organic Concentrates	SG	04702

Control of slugs and snails in gardens.

Dissolve in water and spray around plants or apply as dust. Keep dust off plant foliage, especially under glass, and only use spray when treating seedlings. Repeat treatment as necessary.

F 2   aluminium sulphate + copper sulphate + potassium permanganate

A mixture of metallic salts with a contact action

Nobble Garden Pack	Fieldspray	SL	03498

Control of eggs and newly hatched slugs and snails in gardens.

Dilute as directed and apply to soil with a sprayer or watering can with a fine rose. Cover whole area to be treated and a 3 m (3 yd) barrier. May be used on lawns where rainfall assists penetration into the soil.

F 3   copper sulphate + ferrous sulphate

A mixture of metallic salts

Snail Control	Interpet	SL	02457

Control of pond snails in aquaria and ornamental ponds.

Dilute as directed and add to water; do not exceed stated dose. Reduce dose when sensitive fish present or in very soft water. Snails fall to the bottom in a few hours and should be removed, at the same time changing half the water. Remove carbon from the filtration system before treating aquaria.

F 4 **metaldehyde**

A narcotic chemical killing slugs and snails by dehydration and toxic to man and animals

1 B&Q Slug Killer Blue Mini-Pellets	B&Q	GR	04387
2 Boots Slug Destroyer Mini-Pellets	Boots	GR	02405
3 Cuton Slug Killer Blue Mini-Pellets	Cramphorn	GR	03798
4 Doff Slugoids, Slug Killer Blue Mini-Pellets	Doff	GR	00744
5 Hurrans Garden Centres Blue Mini Slug Pellets	Hurrans	GR	04117
6 ICI Slug Pellets	ICI	GR	01107
7 Mill Slug Killer Blue Mini-Pellets	Mill	GR	04118
8 Murphy Slugit Liquid	Fisons	SL	03633
9 Murphy Slugits	Fisons	GR	03634
10 PBI Slug Mini-Pellets	PBI	GR	02611
11 Secto Slug Kil Pellets	Secto	GR	01907
12 Slug and Snail Killer Pellets	B.H. & B.	GR	01971

Control of slugs and snails in gardens.

Sprinkle pellets evenly around plants, preferably on a warm, moist evening. Pellets contain a mould-inhibitor to increase persistence, an animal repellant to reduce risk of being eaten by pets and a blue dye to discourage uptake by birds. Liquid formulation may be diluted and sprayed over plants (do not harvest edible plants for ten days) [8].

Metaldehyde can kill if eaten. Keep away from children and pets, both in storage and use. Do not leave pellets in heaps on the soil surface, they can be fatal to pets if eaten in quantity.

F 5 **methiocarb**

A carbamate molluscicide and insecticide which kills slugs and snails by a stomach action

PBI Slug Gard	PBI	GR	01963

Control of slugs, snails, leatherjackets, woodlice, millipedes, etc., in gardens.

Sprinkle evenly and thinly around plants at first signs of damage. May also be used in seed drills or planting holes to prevent seed and root damage. Action is not dependent on dry weather conditions.

Keep away from children and pets.

G Domestic Insecticides

GA Products for crawling insects

GA 1	*d*-allethrin + cypermethrin
GA 2	*d*-allethrin + cypermethrin + tetramethrin
GA 3	bioallethrin + permethrin
GA 4	borax
GA 5	borax + carbaryl
GA 6	carbaryl
GA 7	cypermethrin
GA 8	diazinon
GA 9	diazinon + pyrethrins
GA 10	dichlorvos + fenitrothion + tetramethrin
GA 11	dichlorvos + permethrin
GA 12	fenitrothion + tetramethrin
GA 13	gamma-HCH (BHC, lindane)
GA 14	gamma-HCH + pyrethrins/pyrethrum
GA 15	permethrin
GA 16	permethrin + pyrethrins
GA 17	permethrin + tetramethrin
GA 18	*d*-phenothrin
GA 19	pirimiphos-methyl + pyrethrins
GA 20	pyrethrins/pyrethrum

GB Products for flying insects

GB 1	*d*-allethrin
GB 2	*d*-allethrin + cypermethrin + tetramethrin
GB 3	bioallethrin + permethrin
GB 4	diazinon + pyrethrins
GB 5	dichlorvos
GB 6	dichlorvos + permethrin
GB 7	dichlorvos + pyrethrins
GB 8	fenitrothion + tetramethrin
GB 9	permethrin + pyrethrins
GB 10	permethrin + tetramethrin
GB 11	pirimiphos-methyl + pyrethrins
GB 12	pyrethrins/pyrethrum

GC Moth-proofing products

GC 1	gamma-HCH + permethrin
GC 2	gamma-HCH + pyrethrins
GC 3	permethrin

GA Products for crawling insects

GA 1 *d*-allethrin + cypermethrin

A pyrethroid insecticide mixture combining fast knock-down and residual activity

Vapona Ant & Crawling Insect
Spray   Nicholas   RH   H3593

Control of ants, cockroaches, fleas, silverfish, woodlice and other crawling insect pests indoors.

Spray over pests, onto surfaces where pests crawl or hide, or obtain flushing action by spraying into nests and hiding places. Chemical remains active for several weeks. Before spraying carpets, etc., test spray on an inconspicuous part of the material.

Extremely dangerous to fish; remove or cover fish tanks before spraying.

GA 2 *d*-allethrin + cypermethrin + tetramethrin

A pyrethroid insecticide mixture combining fast knock-down and residual activity

see also under **Products for flying insects** (GB)

Raid Ant & Crawling Insect Killer   Johnson Wax   AE   H3001

Control of ants, cockroaches, silverfish, woodlice, beetles, spiders and other crawling insects in the home.

Use as a direct contact or a surface spray.

GA 3 **bioallethrin + permethrin**

A pyrethroid insecticide mixture combining fast knock-down and residual activity

see also under **Crop insecticides** (AA), **Greenhouse insecticides** (CA), **House plant chemicals** (D), **Products for flying insects** (GB)

1 Spraydex Insect Killer   Spraydex   RH   H3834
2 Spraydex Houseplant Spray   Spraydex   RH   H3540
3 Vapona Ant & Crawling Insect
   Killer   Nicholas   AE   H3596

Control of ants, cockroaches, fleas, silverfish, woodlice and other crawling insect pests indoors.

Spray directly at insects exposed on surfaces, onto surfaces where pests crawl or hide, or obtain flushing action by spraying into nests and hiding places. Repeat as necessary. Before spraying carpets, etc., test spray on an inconspicuous part of the material; do not spray heavily on plastics or polished surfaces [3].

Do not spray on food or surfaces which come into contact with food. Extremely dangerous to fish; remove or cover fish tanks before spraying.

GA 4 **borax** (sodium tetraborate)
A mineral insecticide particularly effective against ants

1 Nippon Ant Killer Liquid	Synchemicals	LB	01502
2 Rentokil Ant Killer	Rentokil	LB	04312

See entry under **Crop insecticides** (AA 3).

GA 5 **borax + carbaryl**
As previous entry combined with a general purpose insecticide

Boots Ant Killer	Boots	DP	04088

See entry under **Crop insecticides** (AA 4).

GA 6 **carbaryl**
A contact and stomach-acting carbamate insecticide

see also under **Lawn chemicals** (BA, BE)

1 Dethlac Ant & Insect Powder	Gerhardt	DP	03534
2 Rentokil Ant & Insect Powder	Rentokil	DP	01755

See entry under **Crop insecticides** (AA 6).

GA 7 **cypermethrin**
A contact and stomach-acting pyrethroid insecticide with good residual activity

1 Vapona Ant Pen	Nicholas	AL	H3592
1 Vapona Fly Pen	Nicholas	AL	H3606

Control of ants and other crawling insects [1], of flies, bluebottles, wasps, mosquitoes, midges, ants, silverfish, beetles, cockroaches and other flying and crawling insects [2], in and around the home.

Use as a pen to draw invisible lines on smooth, non-absorbent surfaces where pests are active. Pests contacting the line are killed rapidly. Treatment remains effective for up to two weeks.

GA 8 **diazinon**
A persistent, contact-acting organophosphorus insecticide

1 Cromopest Crawling Insect Killer	Wallace, Cameron	LA	00592
2 Dethlac Insecticidal Lacquer	Gerhardt	LA	00682
3 Doff Antlak	Doff	LA	H3591
4 Secto Ant & Crawling Insect Lacquer	Secto	LA	01897
5 Secto Kil-a-Line	Secto	LA	H3631

Control of ants, beetles, cockroaches, silverfish, woodlice and other crawling insects, also of flies and wasps, in and around the home.

Spray [1–4], or paint [5], lacquer onto hard, non-absorbent surfaces where pests are active. Insects are killed by absorbing the chemical as they crawl over the treated strip. Treatment remains effective for up to six months.

Do not apply to surfaces on which food is stored, prepared or eaten.

GA 9 diazinon + pyrethrins

A combination of a residual organophosphorus and a contact pyrethrum insecticide

see also under **Products for flying insects** (GB)

Rentokil Insectrol   Rentokil   AE   01754

Control of crawling and flying insects indoors.

Apply as a direct contact or a space spray or as a surface treatment to kill insects crawling over treated surface for up to six months.

GA 10 dichlorvos + fenitrothion + tetramethrin

An insecticide mixture combining contact, ingested, fumigant and fast knock-down activity

Keen Superkill Ant & Roach
    Exterminator   Keen   AE   02352

Control of ants, cockroaches and other crawling insects indoors.

Use as a direct contact or a surface spray.

GA 11 dichlorvos + permethrin

An insecticide mixture combining contact, fumigant and residual activity

Secto Household Flea Killer   Secto   AE   03648

Control of fleas, cockroaches, silverfish, spiders, ants and other crawling insects indoors, also of flies, wasps, moths and other flying insects.

Apply to soft furnishings, carpets, on and around pet bedding and sleeping quarters or other places where pests are active. Treatment remains active for several months. Test spray a small area before using on delicate fabrics, or on polished or plastic surfaces. May also be used as a space spray.

GA 12 fenitrothion + tetramethrin

A combination of an organophosphorus and a pyrethroid insecticide with contact and some residual activity

see also under **Products for flying insects** (GB)

| 1 | Doom Ant & Crawling Insect Killer | Napa | AE | H1853 |
| 2 | Rentokil Ant & Crawling Insect Killer | Rentokil | AE | H2177 |

Control of ants, cockroaches, beetles, earwigs, silverfish and other crawling insects indoors.

Use as a direct contact or a surface spray or to flush insects out of nests and hiding places. Treatment remains active for many weeks.

GA 13 gamma-HCH (BHC, lindane)

A contact and stomach acting organochlorine insecticide

see also under **Crop insecticides** (AA)

| 1 | Doff Ant Killer | Doff | DP | 00739 |
| 2 | Doom Ant & Insect Powder | Napa | DP | H2392 |

Control of ants, cockroaches, earwigs, spiders, silverfish, woodlice and other crawling insects indoors and in the garden.

Apply dust where pests are active.

GA 14 gamma-HCH + pyrethrins/pyrethrum

A combination of gamma-HCH with a contact-acting pyrethrum insecticide

see also under **Crop insecticides** (AA) **Moth-proofing products** (GC)

1	Ant Killer	B.H. & B.	DP	00100
2	Doom Fleakiller	Napa	AE	H1444
3	Rentokil Flea Killer	Rentokil	AE	H2178
4	Secto Extra Strength Ant Killer Powder	Secto	DP	00816
5	Secto House & Garden Powder	Secto	DP	01901
6	Secto Insect Killer Powder	Secto	DP	01902

Control of ants, beetles, cockroaches, earwigs, silverfish and other crawling insects in home or garden [1, 4–6], of fleas in the home [2, 3].

Dust powder into places where pests active [1, 4–6]. For up to three months control of fleas spray carpets, curtains, pet baskets, soft furnishings, cracks between floorboards, etc., where fleas and flea larvae are found [2, 3].

Do not apply on animals. Do not apply to surfaces which come into contact with food.

GA 15 permethrin

A contact-acting pyrethroid insecticide with good residual activity

see also under **Crop insecticides** (AA), **Greenhouse insecticides** (CA), **House plant chemicals** (D), **Moth-proofing products** (GC)

1 Johnson's Household Flea Powder	Johnson's Vet.	DP	H2240
2 Secto Flea-Free Insecticidal Rug & Carpet Freshener	Secto	DP	H2445
3 Vapona Ant & Crawling Insect Powder	Nicholas	DP	H3595

Control of fleas in rugs and carpets [2], of fleas in carpets, soft furnishings and pet bedding and of ants and other crawling insects in and around the home [1], of ants, beetles, cockroaches, silverfish, woodlice, fleas, bed-bugs and other crawling insects in and around the home [3].

Dust over carpets and rugs and leave for 30 minutes before vacuum cleaning [2]. Leave for one hour or overnight before brushing off or vacuum cleaning [1]. Dust freely along ant and other insect tracks and into cracks and crevices where pests are likely to hide; may be used on bedding and furnishings [1, 3].

Extremely dangerous to fish; remove or cover fish tanks. Do not apply directly to animals.

GA 16 permethrin + pyrethrins

A pyrethroid insecticide mixture combining fast knock-down and residual activity

see also under **Products for flying insects** (GB)

1 Johnson's Household Flea Spray	Johnson's Vet.	AE	H2290
2 PBI Kybosh	PBI	AE	H3022

Control of dog and cat fleas on carpets, soft furnishings and pet bedding and of ants, beetles, cockroaches, earwigs, silverfish, woodlice and other crawling insects in and around the home.

Use as a contact spray or spray carpets, etc., and cracks and crevices where pests are likely to hide. Repeat weekly or as required. Test spray a small area before using on delicate fabrics, polished or plastic surfaces [1], or wall coverings [2].

Extremely dangerous to fish; remove or cover fish tanks. Do not apply directly to animals.

GA 17 permethrin + tetramethrin

A pyrethroid insecticide mixture combining fast knock-down and residual activity

see also under **Products for flying insects** (GB)

Nippon Ant & Crawling Insect
  Killer   Synchemicals   AE   03039

Control of ants, cockroaches and other crawling insects in and
around the home.

Use as a surface spray as soon as pests appear and spray cracks,
corners, doorsteps, window ledges, etc., where pests hide. Avoid
heavy applications on soft furnishings, carpets and polished
surfaces.

Extremely dangerous to fish; remove or cover fish bowls or tanks.

GA 18   *d*-phenothrin

A pyrethroid insecticide with good persistence suitable for use on
carpets against fleas

Sergeants Rug Patrol   Robins   DP   H2107

Control of dog and cat fleas and ticks and their eggs on carpets,
etc.

Sprinkle powder evenly on carpets, rugs and other upholstery and
leave for 30 minutes (two hours if ticks present) before vacuuming.
Product includes a carpet freshener.

GA 19   pirimiphos-methyl + pyrethrins

An insecticide mixture with fast knock-down and contact activity

see also under **Crop insecticides** (AA), **Greenhouse insecticides**
(CA), **House plant chemicals** (D), **Products for flying insects** (GB)

Waspend   ICI   AE   H0516

Control of wasps, flies, mosquitoes, midges and other flying insects,
also of cockroaches, spiders, ants, silverfish, beetles and other
crawling insects indoors.

Apply as a direct contact or as a space spray. Product retains
activity for some time when sprayed on surfaces.

GA 20   pyrethrins/pyrethrum

A non-persistent, contact-acting insecticide based on extracts of
pyrethrum flowers

see also under **Crop insecticides** (AA), **Greenhouse insecticides**
(CA), **House plant chemicals** (D), **Products for flying insects** (GB)

1 Bio Friendly Anti-Ant Duster	PBI	DP	00098
2 Flit Flying & Crawling Insect Killer Aerosol	Agropharm	AE	H2066
3 Fortefog	Agropharm	AE	H2558
4 Py Powder	Synchemicals	DP	02809
5 Py Spray Garden Insect Killer	Synchemicals	LI	02810

Control of ants in the home and garden [1], of ants, cockroaches, silverfish, flies, wasps and other insect pests in and around the home [2 – 5], and in the garden [4, 5].

Apply as a space or contact spray [2, 3, 5], dust onto insects or into nests and hiding places [1, 4]. Dusting of dustbins prevents fly breeding [4].

GB Products for flying insects

GB 1 *d*-allethrin

A contact-acting pyrethroid insecticide with fast knock-down activity

Floret Fast Knock-Down Fly Killer   Reckitt   AE   04123

Control of flies and wasps indoors.

Apply as a space spray. Close doors and windows and spray into the air for 3–5 seconds. Keep room closed for ten minutes.

GB 2 *d*-allethrin + cypermethrin + tetramethrin

A pyrethroid insecticide mixture combining fast knock-down and good residual activity

see also under **Products for crawling insects** (GA)

Raid Fly & Wasp Killer   Johnson Wax   AE   H3000

Control of flies, wasps, mosquitoes, gnats, moths and other flying insects in the home.

Use as a direct contact or a space spray.

GB 3 bioallethrin + permethrin

A mixture of fast-acting contact pyrethroid insecticides

see also under **Crop insecticides** (AA), **Greenhouse insecticides** (CA), **House plant chemicals** (D), **Products for crawling insects** (GA)

Vapona Fly Killer Aerosol   Nicholas   AE   H2313

Control of flies, bluebottles, wasps and other flying insects indoors.

Use as a space spray. Spray into air in all directions for 3–5 seconds. May be sprayed in the presence of food when used as directed but do not spray directly on food.

Extremely dangerous to fish; remove or cover fish tanks or bowls before use.

GB 4 diazinon + pyrethrins

A mixture of a residual organophosphorus and a contact pyrethrum insecticide

Rentokil Insectrol	Rentokil	AE	01754

See entry under **Products for crawling insects** (GA 9).

GB 5 dichlorvos

A contact and stomach-acting organophosphorus insecticide with fumigant activity

see also under **Greenhouse insecticides** (CA)

1 Fly-Away Insect Killer	Wallace, Cameron	VP	H1067
2 Secto Slow Release Fly-Killer, Kitchen Size	Secto	VP	H2288
3 Sectovap Flykiller Lantern Living Room Size	Secto	VP	H0932
4 Sectovap Moth Killer	Secto	VP	H0934
5 Sectovap New Minispace	Secto	VP	H0867
6 Ultrasect Strip	Wallace, Cameron	VP	H0957
7 Vapona Fly Killer	Nicholas	VP	H1645
8 Vapona Moth Killer	Nicholas	VP	H0537
9 Vapona Small Space Flykiller	Nicholas	VP	H0536

Control of flies, wasps, moths and many other flying insects, as well as silverfish, spiders, cockroaches, and other crawling insects, in the home [1–3, 5–7, 9], of moths in wardrobes [4, 8].

Expose contents of unit and suspend in an open space, away from open windows. Different sized units suitable for different sizes of room or storage space. Keep product away from direct contact with decorated surfaces, furnishings and fabrics.

Do not use in larders or food cupboards or allow to come into contact with food or cooking utensils.

GB 6 dichlorvos + permethrin

An insecticide mixture combining contact, fumigant and residual activity

see also under **Products for crawling insects** (GA)

Secto Household Flea Killer	Secto	AE	03648

Control of flies, wasps, moths and other flying insects indoors, also of fleas, cockroaches and other crawling insects.

Close doors and windows and apply as a space spray. Keep room closed for at least 15 minutes. May also be used as a surface spray. Do not spray over polished or plastic surfaces or directly onto wallpaper.

GB 7   dichlorvos + pyrethrins

A fast-acting mixture of contact insecticides

Secto Rapid Action Flykiller Liquid	Secto	AE	H0469

Control of flies, bluebottles, mosquitoes, wasps and other flying insects indoors.

Apply as a space spray.

GB 8   fenitrothion + tetramethrin

A combination of organophosphorus and pyrethroid insecticides with contact and residual activity

see also under **Products for crawling insects** (GA)

1 Keen Flying Insect Killer	Keen	AE	03683
2 Keen Flying Insect Killer, Faster Knockdown	Keen	AE	03657
3 Keen Universal Insect Killer	Keen	AE	01130
4 Tox Exterminating Fly Spray	Keen	AE	03243

Control of flies, mosquitoes, wasps and other flying insects indoors.

Apply as a space spray.

GB 9   permethrin + pyrethrins

A pyrethroid insecticide mixture combining fast knock-down and residual activity

see also under **Products for crawling insects** (GB)

1 Johnson's Household Flea Spray	Johnson's Vet.	AE	H2290
2 PBI Kybosh	PBI	AE	H3022

Control of flies, bluebottles, wasps, midges, mosquitoes, moths, daddy-long-legs, flying ants and other flying insects, also of crawling insects, indoors.

Apply as a direct contact spray or as a space spray, first closing doors and windows, then spraying for 3–5 seconds and leaving room closed for ten minutes.

Extremely dangerous to fish; remove or cover fish tanks. Do not apply directly to animals.

GB 10   permethrin + tetramethrin

A pyrethroid insecticide mixture combining fast knock-down and residual activity

see also under **Products for crawling insects** (GA)

1	Ciba-Geigy KO Fly & Wasp Killer	Ciba-Geigy	AE	H3726
2	Doom Tropical Strength Fly & Wasp Killer	Napa	AE	H2478
3	Rentokil Fly & Wasp Killer	Rentokil	AE	H2176
4	Sactif Flying Insect Killer	Lever	AE	H2258
5	Secto Fly Killer	Secto	AE	H3862

Control of flies, wasps and other flying insects indoors.

Apply as a direct contact or a space spray.

Extremely dangerous to fish; remove or cover fish tanks.

GB 11 pirimiphos-methyl + pyrethrins

An insecticide mixture with fast knock-down contact activity

see also under **Crop insecticides** (AA), **Greenhouse insecticides** (CA), **House plant chemicals** (D)

Waspend	ICI	AE	H0516

See entry under **Products for crawling insects** (GA 19).

GB 12 pyrethrins/pyrethrum

A non-persistent, contact-acting insecticide based on extracts of pyrethrum flowers

see also under **Crop insecticides** (AA), **Greenhouse insecticides** (CA), **House plant chemicals** (D), **Products for crawling insects** (GA)

1	Big D Fly & Wasp Killer	Domestic Fillers	AE	00263
2	Cromessol Flying Insect Killer	Wallace, Cameron	AE	00590
3	Cromessol Flying Insect Killer (Unperfumed)	Wallace, Cameron	AE	03395
4	Flit Flying & Crawling Insect Killer Aerosol	Agropharm	AE	H2066
5	Fortefog	Agropharm	AE	H2558
6	Prevent	Agropharm	AE	H2324
7	Py Spray Garden Insect Killer	Synchemicals	LI	02810

Control of flies, wasps, mosquitoes and other flying insects [1–7], and of cockroaches and other crawling insects indoors [4–7]. May also be used on exposed skin to repel mosquitoes, biting flies, sandflies, gnats and midges [6].

Apply as a space spray [1–3], as a contact or space spray [4–7]. May be used on animal bedding but do not apply direct onto animals.

If used on soft furnishings do not handle treated fabric until spray has dried and air thoroughly before use [4, 5]. Cover food before spraying. Dangerous to fish; cover or remove fish bowls.

GC Moth-proofing products

GC 1 gamma-HCH + permethrin

A contact and residual mixture of organochlorine and pyrethroid chemicals

Secto Mothproofer   Secto   AE   H2214

Control of clothes moths and their larvae on woollen materials and furs.

Apply as a protective spray to carpets, soft furnishings and other fabrics before storing. Product is non-staining.

GC 2 gamma-HCH + pyrethrins

A contact and residual mixture of organochlorine and pyrethrum insecticides

see also under **Crop insecticides** (AA), **Products for crawling insects** (GA)

1 Doom Mothproofer   Napa   AE   H0588
2 Rentokil Carpet Beetle Killer
   & Mothproofer   Rentokil   AE   H2179

Control of clothes moths, their larvae (woolly bears) and carpet beetles on carpets and fabrics.

Apply as a protective spray to carpets, curtains, clothing, cupboards, drawers, etc. Treatment provides protection for six months.

GC 3 permethrin

A contact-acting pyrethroid insecticide with good residual activity

see also under **Crop insecticides** (AA), **Greenhouse insecticides** (CA), **House plant chemicals** (D), **Products for crawling insects** (GA)

Vapona Moth Proofer Aerosol   Nicholas   AE   H3597

Control of clothes moths and their larvae on clothing, blankets, carpets and furnishings and of carpet beetles and larvae (woolly bears) in carpets and clothing.

Apply a protective spray to both sides of articles, paying special attention to folds. Spray clothes (clean and free from grease spots) before storing. Internal surfaces of drawers and wardrobes may also be treated. To protect against carpet beetle spray a strip 30 cm (12 in) wide round edges and under infrequently moved furniture.

Do not use on furs or foam-backed carpets. Do not spray heavily on plastics or polished surfaces. Before treating delicate or expensive fabrics test spray on an inconspicuous area. Extremely dangerous to fish; cover or remove fish tanks before spraying.

H Animal and Bird Repellents

H 1   aluminium ammonium sulphate
H 2   methyl-nonyl ketone (undecan-2-one)
H 3   naphthalene
H 4   pepper dust
H 5   quassia

H 1   aluminium ammonium sulphate

A bitter-tasting metallic salt

1 Curb Garden Pack	Sphere	SP	03983
2 Scoot	Garotta	SP	03706
3 Stay-Off	Synchemicals	SP	02091

Repels damaging birds and animals [1–3], including moles [2].

Dissolve powder in water and use as spray or apply as dust to seeds, bulbs, etc.

Wash treated fruit and vegetables before use.

H 2   methyl-nonyl ketone (undecan-2-one)

A strong-smelling organic crystalline substance

Get-Off-My-Garden	Get-Off-My-Garden	RH	04573

Repels cats and dogs.

Sprinkle crystals as a protective treatment on paths, patios and yards and around lawns and plant beds.

H 3   naphthalene

A fumigant hydrocarbon solid

1 Scent-Off Buds	Synchemicals	XX	02907
2 Scent-Off Pellets	Synchemicals	PT	01888

Protects from fouling by dogs and cats.

Apply to fouled areas after cleansing and repeat treatment approximately monthly.

H 4   pepper dust

A plant product irritating but harmless to animals

1 PBI Pepper Dust	PBI	DP	01569
2 Pepper Dust	Synchemicals	DP	01570
3 Scram	De Witt	DP	03469

Repels dogs and cats.

Apply liberally to plants and soil. Repeat the application after rain.

H 5   quassia

An extract from Quassia wood chips

1 Cat-Off	Fieldspray	RH	04400
2 Dog-Off	Fieldspray	RH	04401
3 Garden Hoppit	Fieldspray	SL	04398
4 Garden Hoppit Ready-to-Use	Fieldspray	RH	04399

Repels cats [1], dogs [2], rabbits, deer and birds [3, 4].

Spray where cats are an habitual nuisance [1], on gateposts and other sniffing and marking points for dogs [2], over flowers, fruit, vegetables and other plants requiring protection [3, 4]. Requires six hours drying time.

Treated food crops may be eaten 24 hours after treatment [3, 4].

J   Rat and Mouse Killers

J 1	alphachloralose
J 2	brodifacoum
J 3	bromadiolone
J 4	calciferol + difenacoum
J 5	chlorphacinone
J 6	coumatetralyl
J 7	difenacoum
J 8	sulphur
J 9	warfarin

J 1   alphachloralose

A non-cumulative, narcotic mouse killer

Rentokil Alphakil Mouse Killer	Rentokil	RB	01722

Control of mice indoors.

Pour contents of sachet into shallow containers and place where mice are active. Inspect frequently and replace until no more bait taken. Mice usually die within 24 hours of eating bait. Best used when floor temperature below 16°C. Prevent access to bait by children and domestic animals. Do not use outside.

J 2   brodifacoum

A single-dose, anti-coagulant mouse killer

Mouser	ICI	RB	03213

Control of mice on domestic premises.

Place ready-to-use bait box where mice are running or feeding. When mouse activity has ceased place bait box in a plastic bag, seal and dispose of in dustbin.

J 3 bromadiolone

1 Bromadeth Rat & Mouse Killer	Gerhardt	RB	03515
2 Rentokil Biotrol Plus Outdoor Rat Killer	Rentokil	RB	02936
3 Rentokil Mouse Killer System	Rentokil	RB	02994
4 Rentokil Rodine C Rat & Mouse Killer	Rentokil	RB	03318

Control of mice and rats indoors and outdoors [1, 4], of rats outdoors [2], of mice indoors [3].

Place baits in shallow containers in rodent runs, inspect frequently and replenish until feeding ceases; protect from wind and rain if used outside [1, 4]. Product specially treated for use in damp situations [2]. Use in conjunction with bait boxes supplied [3]. Prevent access to baits by children and domestic animals.

J 4 calciferol + difenacoum

A mouse killer mixture combining two modes of action

Sorexa CD Mouse Killer	Sorex	RB	03514

Control of mice (including warfarin-resistant mice) on domestic premises.

Pour contents of sachets onto cards or tin lids and place where mice are active. Inspect baits and replace where taken. Mice die 3–10 days after taking bait.

J 5 chlorophacinone

A single-dose, anti-coagulant rat and mouse killer

Drat Rat & Mouse Bait	B.H. & B.	RB	00764

Control of rats and mice.

Place heaps of bait in holes or along runs at places not often disturbed. Inspect 7–10 days later and replenish or remove as necessary. Prevent access to baits by children and domestic animals.

J 6 coumatetralyl

A cumulative, anti-coagulant rat and mouse killer

1 Racumin Mouse Bait	PBI	RB	01678
2 Racumin Rat Bait	PBI	RB	01680

Control of rats and mice.

Place heaps of bait near holes or where traces of rats or mice are found. Replenish until feeding ceases. Protect baits from weather and prevent access by children or domestic animals. To encourage acceptance of bait by rats see that clean drinking water is available.

J 7   difenacoum

A cumulative, anti-coagulant rat and mouse killer

Ratak   ICI   RB   02586

Control of rats and mice, including warfarin-resistant types.

Place pellets on pieces of card at four or more sites where rodents are feeding. Check daily and replace baits which have been eaten. Two or more feeds are needed for control, which may take up to two weeks. Prevent access to baits by children, animals and birds. Ensure a minimum choice of alternative food for rodents.

J 8   sulphur

A combustible solid which produces a toxic gas on ignition

Murphy Mole Smokes   Fisons   FU   03615

Control of moles, mice and rats in the garden.

Dig into new mole hills to find tunnels. Light cartridge, insert into hole after smoke emission has started and cover with soil or turf. Repeat when any new holes or hills are found.

J 9   warfarin

A cumulative, anti-coagulant rat and mouse killer

1 Warfarin 0.5% Concentrate   B.H. & B.   CB   02325
2 Warfarin Ready Mixed Bait   B.H. & B.   RB   02333

Control of rats and mice.

Mix concentrate with oatmeal, flour, bread crumbs or other suitable material as directed, or use ready-mixed bait, and place on tin lids or other shallow containers where rodents are feeding. Inspect at frequent intervals and replenish as necessary. Poison may take 5–14 days to act. Prevent access to baits by children and domestic animals.

K Miscellaneous Products

KA Rooting hormones
- KA 1   4-indol-3-ylbutyric acid (IBA) + 1-naphthylacetic acid (NAA) + thiram
- KA 2   1-naphthylacetic acid (NAA) + captan
- KA 3   1-naphthylacetic acid (NAA) + dichlorophen
- KA 4   1-naphthylacetic acid (NAA) + thiram

KB Growth retardants
- KB 1   dikegulac
- KB 2   maleic hydrazide

KC Fruit setting products
- KC 1   naphthyloxy acetic acid

KD Non-chemical insect controls
- KD 1   biological control
- KD 2   glue traps
- KD 3   pheromone lure and trap

KA Rooting hormones

KA 1   4-indol-3-ylbutyric acid (IBA) + 1-naphthylacetic acid (NAA) + thiram

A combination of two rooting hormones with a protective fungicide

Boots Hormone Rooting Powder   Boots   DP 01067

Promotion of rooting of all types of cutting and control of stem rot in cuttings and damping off in seedlings.

Dip base of cuttings into powder and plant in normal way. Sprinkle lightly over seeds before covering with soil to protect against damping off.

KA 2   1-naphthylacetic acid (NAA) + captan

A combination of a rooting hormone and a protective fungicide

1 Doff Hormone Rooting Powder	Doff	DP	01065
2 Keriroot	ICI	DP	01137
3 M & B Strike	May & Baker	DP	04430
4 Murphy Hormone Rooting Powder	Fisons	DP	03618
5 Synchemicals (ex Corry's) Rooting Powder	Synchemicals	DP	00584

Promotion of rooting in all types of cutting and protection against stem rot.

Dip base of cuttings into powder and plant in normal way.

KA 3 1-naphthylacetic acid (NAA) + dichlorophen

A combination of a rooting hormone and a protective fungicide

Bio Roota   PBI   SL   00271

Promotion of rooting on all types of cutting and protection against basal rot.

Dip base of prepared cuttings into ready-to-use solution and plant in normal way.

KA 4 1-naphthylacetic acid (NAA) + thiram

A combination of a rooting hormone and a protective fungicide

Secto Hormone Rooting Powder   Secto   DP   01001

Promotion of rooting of all types of cutting and protection against basal rot.

Dip base of cutting into powder and plant in normal way.

KB Growth retardants

KB 1 dikegulac

A plant growth regulator which inhibits the growth of leading shoots

Cutlass   ICI   SL   00617

Control of shoot growth of hedge plants and many ornamental shrubs.

Spray thoroughly, ensuring that all foliage is completely wetted, when plants are growing well with a good cover of green foliage (usually from late May onwards), after trimming to the desired shape. In hot weather spraying is best delayed until evening. Do not use more than once in season. Do not use on yew, box, viburnum, roses (except *Rosa rugosa*) or myrobalan plum; see label for permitted species.

When used as directed product presents no risk to domestic animals or wildlife, including nesting birds.

KB 2 maleic hydrazide

A plant growth regulator which suppresses growth by temporarily stopping cell division at the shoot tips

Stop Gro G8   Kent Country   SL   02029

Inhibition of growth of rough and medium grass and control of shoot growth of evergreen hedge plants.

To control grass growth apply evenly with a sprayer or watering can when the grass is growing actively. Best results are achieved when growth is started in April–May, with a repeat treatment when growth recommences. Need for mowing is reduced for up to six weeks. On hedges apply as an overall spray when hedge in active growth. Rain within eight hours after application may reduce effectiveness.

Avoid drift onto nearby vegetables, flowers or other garden plants.

KC Fruit setting products

KC 1 naphthyloxy acetic acid

A plant growth regulator which increases fruit setting of tomatoes

Synchemicals Tomato Setting
Spray   Synchemicals   AE   03735

Increasing fruit set of greenhouse tomatoes (may also be used on outdoor tomatoes).

Commence spraying when first six flowers on the first truss are open, applying further sprays as flowers appear on other trusses. Treat flowering trusses once only. Spray from at least 30 cm (12 in) away and direct spray at flowering trusses, avoiding surrounding foliage.

KD Non-chemical insect control

KD 1 biological control

Biological control of caterpillars with *Bacillus thuringiensis* is covered by the Pesticide Regulations and is dealt with under the Crop insecticides section (entry AA 1). For other biological control agents which can be used in the greenhouse against pests such as red spider mite, whitefly, mealybug, aphids and scale insects see the section on Biological control on page 33.

KD 2 glue traps

1 Bio Friendly Greenhouse
   Fly Catcher   PBI   XX   —
2 Dethtrap Whitefly Catcher   Gerhardt   XX   —

Control of whitefly, greenfly, blackfly, thrips, midges and other flying insects in greenhouses and conservatories.

KD 3 pheromone lure + trap

A sex attractant luring codling moths into a sticky trap

Trappit Codling Moth Traps   Agralan   XX   —

Monitoring and trapping of male codling moth on apples and pears.

Assemble trap, place attractant capsule on sticky insert, slide insert into trap and hang in selected tree. Trap should be in place by mid-May or at full bloom, whichever is earlier. Change base and lure after five weeks. Use one trap per five trees. Additional spraying may be necessary with heavy infestations.

Glossary

acaricide – a chemical which kills mites.

algicide – a chemical which kills algae.

annual weed – a weed which completes its life-cycle in less than a year and dies after producing seed.

anti-coagulant rodenticide – a chemical which kills rats and mice through the prevention of blood clotting.

aphicide – a chemical active mainly against aphids.

beneficial insects – includes pollinating insects, such as bees etc., and insects which act as predators or parasites on pest species.

biological control – the use of introduced predators, parasites or diseases to control pests and weeds.

broad spectrum – a pesticide effective against a wide range of pests, diseases or weeds.

caterpillar – the larva of a moth, butterfly or sawfly.

contact insecticide – a chemical which kills insects on contact.

contact pre-emergence treatment – application of a non-persistent contact weedkiller during the period before the crop seedlings have emerged to kill any weed seedlings which have emerged before the crop.

contact weedkiller – a chemical which kills those parts of a plant with which it makes contact.

crop plant – in this book refers to any type of desirable garden plant.

curative fungicide – a chemical capable of curing a fungus disease which is already established in a plant.

emulsifiable concentrate – a concentrated formulation of chemical which forms an emulsion when mixed with water.

eelworms – see *nematodes*.

emulsion – a suspension of minute droplets of oil in water.

flocculating agent – a substance which causes suspended particles to aggregate and sink.

foliar activity – having an effect through the leaves.

formulation – the way in which active chemicals are prepared for application by the user.

frill – a series of shallow, overlapping, downwardly directed cuts around the base of a tree trunk into which chemical is applied.

fumigant – a chemical which acts in vapour form.

gel – a thick, jelly-like formulation.

growth retardant – a chemical used to slow down the growth of plants without killing them.

grub – the larva of beetles and various other insects.

harvest interval – the period which must be allowed after the last application of a chemical before a crop can be safely harvested.

honeydew – a sticky secretion exuded by various sap-sucking insects.

hormone weedkillers – see *synthetic plant growth regulators.*

HSE Number – the number under which a pesticide is registered by the Health and Safety Executive.

ingested insecticide (stomach-acting) – a type of insecticide which has to be eaten to be effective.

larva – the crawling stage which hatches out from the eggs of beetles, butterflies, moths and various other flying insects.

leaching – the process whereby chemicals are washed through the soil by rainfall or irrigation.

MAFF Number – the number under which a pesticide is registered by MAFF.

molluscicide – a chemical used to kill slugs and snails.

narcotic – a chemical with a deadening effect.

necrosis – the browning and drying up of plant tissues.

nematodes – minute, non-segmented cylindrical worms which may be parasitic on plants and animals. Plant nematodes are often called eelworms.

non-selective weedkiller – a chemical capable of killing both weeds and crop plants, useful for non-crop areas but needing carefully directed application if used in crops.

nymph – a young stage in the life-cycle of certain types of insect, such as scale insects.

organochlorine – a class of chlorine-containing organic chemicals effective as insecticides, some of which are very persistent.

organophosphorus – a class of phosphorus-containing organic chemicals effective as insecticides, generally with considerable mammalian toxicity.

parasites – organisms which live in or on other 'host' organisms and feed at the expense of the host.

perennial weed – a weed persisting for several years, usually with underground food storage organs.

pesticide – any chemical used for the control of insect and other pests, plant diseases or weeds; pesticide legislation also covers various chemicals which in the strict sense are not pesticides, such as animal repellants and plant growth regulators.

pheromones – natural chemicals produced by insects which influence feeding, reproductive or other behaviour.

plant growth regulator – a chemical which influences the growth of plants, generally by either retardation or stimulation.

post-emergence treatment (with weed-killers) – a treatment applied after the emergence of crop and weeds; can only be used on crops unaffected by the chemical concerned.

predators – insects, mites and other animals which prey on other species and can be beneficial when they prey on pests.

pre-emergence treatment – a treatment applied to the soil before the emergence of a crop which kills seedlings as they germinate; established weeds are generally little affected.

protective fungicide – a chemical which protects plants from infection with fungus diseases, usually by killing the spores, but cannot cure disease which is already established.

pupa – the usually inactive stage between the larva and the adult stage of butterflies, moths and various other flying insects.

pustule – pimple-like fungal growths on plant surfaces associated with the development of spore-producing bodies.

pyrethroid insecticides – synthetic chemicals related to natural pyrethrins which combine high insecticidal activity and low mammalian toxicity without presenting undesirable residue problems.

rooting hormones – synthetic chemicals related to naturally occurring plant growth regulators which promote the rooting of cuttings.

selective weedkiller – a chemical which kills some types of weed (usually broad-leaved species) without affecting some crop plants (usually grasses), e.g. most lawn weedkillers.

soil-acting weedkiller – a weedkiller taken up by plants mainly via the roots.

soil insecticide – a relatively persistent chemical effective against soil-dwelling insects.

soil sterilant – a treatment which kills insect and other pests, fungal and bacterial disease organisms and some weed seeds in the soil.

stomach-acting insecticide – see *ingested insecticide.*

stylet – the tube-like mouthparts of aphids and other sap-sucking insects.

surfactant – a surface-active compound used in formulating pesticides to assist in making emulsions and suspensions and to act as wetting agents, spreaders etc.

suspension – a dispersion of solid particles of chemical throughout a liquid.

suspension concentrate – a concentrated formulation of chemical consisting of very finely divided particles of solid material together with surfactants which maintain a stable suspension.

synthetic plant growth regulators – a class of weedkillers related to the naturally occurring growth regulating chemicals in plants; they are often known as hormone weedkillers.

systemic – a chemical which is absorbed through one part of a plant, usually the roots, and then moved throughout the plant. To be effective a lethal dose of a *systemic insecticide* must be taken up by insects through feeding. *Systemic fungicides* are active within plants and may be curative.

translocated – moved within a plant by the plant's own transport system; a *translocated weedkiller* is one which, after application to the foliage under suitable conditions, is moved downwards and kills the root system.

urea nitrogen – an organic form of nitrogen fertiliser.

weevils – a sub-class of beetles, often flightless.

wettable powder – a powder formulation of a chemical with added surfactant which can be mixed with water to form a suspension suitable for spraying.

Index of active ingredients

(Entry numbers in italics refer to active ingredients in mixtures)

Active ingredient	Entry number
d-allethrin	GB 1
d-allethrin + cypermethrin	GA 1
d-allethrin + cypermethrin + tetramethrin	GA 2, GB 2
alloxydim-sodium	AD 1
alphachloralose	J 1
aluminium ammonium sulphate	H 1
aluminium sulphate	F 1
aluminium sulphate + copper sulphate + potassium permanganate	F 2
aminotriazole – **see** amitrole	
amitrole + atrazine	EA 1
amitrole + atrazine + 2, 4–D	EA 2
amitrole + 2, 4–D + diuron + paraquat	EA 3
amitrole + diquat + paraquat + simazine	EA 4
amitrole + MCPA	EA 5
amitrole + MCPA + simazine	EA 6
amitrole + simazine	EA 7
ammonium sulphamate	AD 2, EA 8
atrazine	*EA 1,2*
atrazine + sodium chlorate	EA 9
Bacillus thuringiensis	AA 1
benazolin + 2, 4–D + dicamba + dichlorophen + dichlorprop + mecoprop	BC 1, BD 1, BE 1
benomyl	AB 1, BB 1, CB 1, D 1
BHC – **see** gamma-HCH	
bioallethrin + permethrin	AA 2, CA 1, D 2, GA 3, GB 3
biological control	KD 1
bitumen	AE 1
borax	AA 3, GA 4
borax + carbaryl	AA 4, GA 5
brodifacoum	J 2
bromadiolone	J 3
bromophos	AA 5, CA 2
bupirimate + pirimicarb + triforine	AC 1
bupirimate + triforine	AB 2
butoxycarboxim	D 3
calciferol + difenacoum	J 4
captan	*KA 2*
captan + gamma-HCH	AC 2
carbaryl	*AA 4,* AA 6, BA 1,2, BE 2,3 *GA 5, GA 6*
carbaryl + rotenone	AA 7

carbendazim	AB 3, BB 2, CB 2
carbendazim + copper oxychloride + permethrin + sulphur	AC 3
carbendazim + quaternary ammonium compounds	EB 1
(chlordane)	AA 8, BE 4
chlorophacinone	J 5
chloroxuron + dichlorophen + ferrous sulphate	BD 2
chloroxuron + ferric sulphate	BD 3
chloroxuron + ferrous sulphate	BD 4
copper oxychloride	AB 4, *AC 3*, CB 3
copper sulphate	AB 5, CB 4, *F 2*
copper sulphate + ferrous sulphate	F 3
coumatetralyl	J 6
cresylic acid – **see** tar acids/tar oils	
cypermethrin	*GA 1,2, GA 7, GB 2*
2, 4–D	*BC 1,* BC 2, *BD 1, BE 1, EA 2,3*
2, 4–D + dicamba	BC 3,4
2, 4–D + dicamba + ferrous sulphate	BC 5, BD 5
2, 4–D + dicamba + mecoprop	EA 10
2, 4–D + dichlorprop	BC 6,7
2, 4–D + dichlorprop + mecoprop	BC 8
2, 4–D + ferrous sulphate	BC 9
2, 4–D + ferrous sulphate + mecoprop	BC 10, BD 6
2, 4–D + mecoprop	BC 11, 12
2, 4–D + 2,3,6-TBA	BC 13
dalapon	AD 3, EA 11
derris – **see** rotenone	
diazinon	GA 8
diazinon + pyrethrins	GA 9, GB 4
dicamba	*BC 1,3,4,5, BD 1, BE 1,5, EA 10*
dicamba + dichlorprop + MCPA	BC 14,15, EA 12
dicamba + MCPA	BC 16
dicamba + MCPA + mecoprop	AD 4, BC 17,18
dichlobenil	AD 5, EA 13
dichlorophen	BB 3,4, *BC 1, BD 1,2,* BD 7,8, *BE 1,* CD 1, EB 2, *KA 3*
dichlorophen + ferrous sulphate	BD 9
dichlorprop	*BC 1,6,7,8,14,15, BD 1, BE 1, EA 12*
dichlorprop + ferrous sulphate + MCPA	BC 19, BD 10
dichlorprop + MCPA	BC 20
dichlorvos	CA 3, GB 5
dichlorvos + fenitrothion + tetramethrin	GA 10
dichlorvos + gamma-HCH + tetramethrin	AA 9, CA 4
dichlorvos + permethrin	GA 11, GB 6
dichlorvos + pyrethrins	GB 7
difenacoum	*J 4,* J 7
dikegulac	KB 1
dimethoate	AA 10, D 4

dimethoate + gamma-HCH + thiram	AC 4, CC 1, D 5
dimethoate + permethrin	AA 11, CA 5
dinocap + permethrin + sulphur + triforine	AC 5
diquat	*EA 4*
diquat + paraquat	AD 6, EA 14
diuron	*EA 3*
diuron + simazine	EA 15
fatty acids	AA 12, CA 6, D 6
fenitrothion	AA 13, *GA 10*
fenitrothion + tetramethrin	GA 12, GB 8
ferric sulphate	*BD 3*
ferrous sulphate	*BC 5,9,10,19*, BC 21, *BD 2,4,5,6, 9,10*, BD 11,12, *F 3*
gamma-HCH (BHC, lindane)	*AA 9*, AA 14, *AC 2,4, CA 4, CC 1, D 5*, GA 13
gamma-HCH + permethrin	GC 1
gamma-HCH + pyrethrins/pyrethrum	AA 15, GA 14, GC 2
gamma-HCH + rotenone + thiram	AC 6
gamma-HCH + tecnazene	CC 2
glue traps	KD 2
glyphosate	AD 7, BC 22, EA 16
grease	AA 16
heptenophos + permethrin	AA 17, CA 7
4-indol-3-ylbutyric acid + 1-naphthylacetic acid + thiram	KA 1
lindane – **see** gamma-HCH	
malathion	AA 18, CA 8
malathion + permethrin	AA 19
maleic hydrazide	KB 2
mancozeb	AB 6, CB 5
MCPA	*AD 4, BC 14,15,16,17,18,19,20, BD 10, EA 5,6,12*
MCPA + mecoprop	BC 23
mecoprop	*AD 4, BC 1,8,10,11,12,17,18,23, BD 1,6, BE 1, EA 10*
mercurous chloride	AB 7
metaldehyde	F 4
methiocarb	F 5
methyl-nonyl ketone – **see** undecan-2-one	
myclobutanil	AB 8
naphthalene	H 3
1-naphthylacetic acid	*KA 1*
1-naphthylacetic acid + captan	KA 2
1-naphthylacetic acid + dichlorophen	KA 3

1-naphthylacetic acid + thiram	KA 4
naphthyloxyacetic acid	KC 1
paraquat	*AD 6, EA 4,14*
pepper dust	H4
permethrin	*AA 2,11,17,19,* AA 20, *AC 3,5,* *CA 1,5,7,* CA 9, *D 2,* D 7, *GA 3,11,* GA 15, *GB 3,6, GC 1,* GC 3
permethrin + pyrethrins	GA 16, GB 9
permethrin + tetramethrin	GA 17, GB 10
pheromone lure and trap	KD 3
phoxim	AA 21
pirimicarb	AA 22, *AC 1,* CA 10
pirimiphos-methyl	AA 23, BA 3, CA 11
pirimiphos-methyl + pyrethrins	AA 24, CA 12, D 8, GA 18, GB 11
propachlor	AD 8
propiconazole	AB 9
pyrazophos	AB 10, D 9
pyrethrum/pyrethrins	*AA 15,24,* AA 25, *CA 12,* CA 13, *D 8, GA 9,14,16,19,* GA 20, *GB 4,7,9,11,* GB 12, *GC 2*
pyrethrum/pyrethrins + resmethrin	AA 26, CA 14, D 10
pyrethrum + rotenone	AA 27
quassia	H5
quassia + rotenone (derris)	AA 28, CA 15
quaternary ammonium compounds	CD 2
resmethrin	*AA 26, CA 14, D 10*
rotenone	*AA 7,27,28,* AA 29, *AC 6, CA 15,* CA 16
rotenone (derris) + sulphur	AC 7, CC 3
simazine	AD 9, *EA 3,4,6,7,15,* EA 17
sodium chlorate	*EA 9,* EA 18
sulphur	AB 11, *AC 3,5,7, CC 3,* CD 3, J 8
tannic acid	EC 1
tar acids/tar oils	AA 30, AC 8, AE 2, BC 24, CD 4, BD 13, EB 3
2,3,6-TBA	*BC 13*
tecnazene	*CC 2*
tetramethrin	*AA 9, CA 4, GA 2,10,12,17,* *GB 2, 8,10*
thiophanate-methyl	AB 12, BB 5, CB 6
thiram	*AC 4,6, CC 1, D 5, KA 4*
Trichoderma viride	AB 13
triforine	*AB 2, AC 1,5*
undecan-2-one	H 2
warfarin	J 9
wax	AE 3

Index of products

Boots Total Lawn Treatment	BC 1, BD 1, BE 1
Bordeaux Mixture	AB 5, CB 4
Bromadeth Rat & Mouse Killer	J 3
Bug Gun for Fruit & Vegetables	AA 25, CA 13
Bug Gun for Roses & Flowers	AA 25, CA 13
Calomel Dust	AB 7
Casoron G4	AD 5, EA 13
Cat-Off	H 5
Cheshunt Compound	AB 5, CB 4
Ciba-Geigy KO Fly & Wasp Killer	GB 10
Clean-Up	AC 8, BD 13, CD 4, EB 3
Concentrated Selective Weed Killer	BC 11
Cookes Liquid Sodium Chlorate Weedkiller	EA 18
Cookes Sodium Chlorate Weedkiller	EA 18
Corry's Fruit Tree Grease	AA 16
Cromopest Crawling Insect Killer	GA 8
Cromopest Flying Insect Killer	GB 12
Cromopest Flying Insect Killer (Unperfumed)	GB 12
Curb Garden Pack	H 1
Cutlass	KB 1
Cuton Ant Powder	AA 14
Cuton Slug Killer Blue Mini Pellets	F 4
Dax Root Out	AD 2
Dee Weed	EA 1
Derris Dust	AA 29, CA 16
Dethlac Ant & Insect Powder	AA 6, GA 6
Dethlac Insecticidal Lacquer	GA 8
Dethtrap	KD 2
Dipel	AA 1
Dithane 945	AB 6, CB 5
Doff Ant Killer	AA 14, GA 13
Doff Antlak	GA 7
Doff Calomel Dust	AB 7
Doff Derris Dust	AA 29, CA 16
Doff Fruit & Vegetable Insecticide Spray	AA 25
Doff Hormone Rooting Powder	KA 2
Doff Lawn Spot-Weeder	BC 6
Doff Lawn Weedkiller	BC 6
Doff Rose & Flower Insecticide Spray	AA 25
Doff Slugoids Slug Killer Blue Mini-pellets	F 4
Doff Sodium Chlorate	EA 18
Doff Systemic Insecticide	AA 10
Dog-Off	H 5
Doom Ant & Crawling Insect Killer	GA 12
Doom Ant & Insect Powder	GA 13
Doom Fleakiller	GA 14
Doom Garden Insect Killer Aerosol	AA 26, CA 14
Doom Greenhouse & Garden Insect Killer	AA 26, CA 14
Doom Moth Proofer	GC 2
Doom Tropical Strength Fly & Wasp Killer	GB 10

Drat Rat & Mouse Bait	J 5
Fertosan Slug & Snail Killer	F 1
Fisons Antkiller	AA 21
Fisons Autumn Extra	BD 12
Fisons Evergreen 90	BC 23
Fisons Insect Spray for Houseplants	D 7
Fisons Lawn Sand	BD 12
Fisons Lawn Spot Weeder	BC 3
Fisons Lawncare Liquid	BC 18
Fisons Mosskil Extra	BD 12
Fisons Path Weeds Killer	EA 6
Fisons Problem Weeds Killer	EA 5
Fisons Soil Pest Killer	AA 21
Fisons Turf Weeds Killer	BC 16
Flit Flying & Crawling Insect Killer Aerosol	GA 20, GB 12
Floret Fast Knock Down Fly Killer	GB 1
Fly-Away Insect Killer	GB 5
Fortefog	GA 20, GB 12
FS Total Weedkiller	EA 1
Fumite General Purpose Insecticide Smoke Cones	CA 11
Fumite Tecnalin Smoke Cones	CC 2
Fumite Whitefly Cones	CA 9
Fungo	BD 7, CD 1, EB 2
Gamma BHC Garden Spray	AA 14
Garden Hoppit	H 5
Garden Hoppit Ready-to-Use	H 5
Garden Jack House & Garden Disinfectant	CD 2
Gateway Lawn Feed & Weedkiller	BC 20
Gateway Lawn Feed with Weedkiller	BC 12
Gateway Mosskiller With Fertilizer	BD 12
Gateway Pest Spray for Fruit & Vegetables	AA 25, CA 13
Gateway Pest Spray for Roses & Flowers	AA 25, CA 13
Gateway Weed Spray for Lawns	BC 11
Gem Lawn Sand	BD 12
Gem Lawn Weed & Feed	BC 12
Gem Lawn Weed & Feed + Mosskiller	BC 10, BD 6
Gem Lawn Weed & Feed 4	BC 12
Gem Sodium Chlorate	EH 18
Get-Off-My-Garden	H 2
Good Life Lawn Weed & Feed	BC 9
Greenaway for Ponds	EC 1
Greenfly Aerosol Spray	AA 18, CA 8
Greenfly Spray	AA 27
Greenscape Weedkiller	AD 7, EA 16
Green Sulphur	AB 11
Green Sulphur Powder	AB 11
Green-Up Feed & Weed + Mosskiller	BC 10, BD 6
Green-Up Lawn Feed & Weed	BC 4
Green-Up Mossfree	BD 11

Green-Up Weedfree Lawn Weedkiller	BC 3
Green-Up Weedfree Spot Weedkiller	BC 3
Growing Success Slug Killer	F 1
Hurrans Garden Centres Blue Mini Slug Pellets	F 4
Hytrol	EA 3
ICI Antkiller	AA 23, CA 11
ICI Club Root Control	AB 7
ICI Derris Dust	AA 29, CA 16
ICI Mosskiller for Lawns	BD 12
ICI Slug Pellets	F 4
ICI Sodium Chlorate	EA 18
J Arthur Bowers Feed & Weed	BC 20
J Arthur Bowers Feed & Weed + Mosskiller	BC 19, BD 10
J Arthur Bowers Lawn Food With Weedkiller	BC 12
J Arthur Bowers Lawn Sand	BD 12
J Arthur Bowers Moss Killer	BD 9
Jeyes Fluid	AC 8, CD 4
Johnsons Household Flea Powder	GA 15
Johnsons Household Flea Spray	GA 16, GB 9
Keen Flying Insect Killer	GB 8
Keen Flying Insect Killer, Faster Knockdown	GB 8
Keen Superkill Ant & Roach Exterminator	GA 10
Keen Universal Insect Killer	GB 8
Keriguards	D 4
Keriroot	KA 2
Kerispray	D 8
Lawnsman Liquid Weed & Feed	BC 15
Lawnsman Mosskiller	BD 2
Lawnsman Weed & Feed	BC 4
Lever Sodium Chlorate	EA 18
M&B Lawn Feed & Weed Granules	BC 12
M&B Lawn Spot Weed Granules	BC 11
M&B Liquid Club Root Control	AB 12
M&B Path & Drive Weedkiller	EA 7
M&B Strike	KA 2
M&B Supergreen & Weed	BC 12
M&B Supergreen Feed Weed & Mosskiller	BC 10, BD 6
M&B Supertox Lawn Weed Spray	BC 11
M&B Systemic Fungicide Liquid	AB 12, BB 5, CB 6
M&B Total Weedkiller Granules	EA 15
M&B Weed Out	AD 1
Malathion Dust	AA 18, CA 8
Malathion 50 Liquid Spray	AA 18, CA 8
Maxicrop Mosskiller & Lawn Tonic	BD 12
Medo	AE 2

Mill Lawn Sand	BD 12
Mill Slug Killer Blue Mini-Pellets	F 4
Moss Gun for Lawns & Paths	BD 7, EB 2
Mouser	J 2
Murphy Ant Killer Powder	AA 14
Murphy Combined Seed Dressing	AC 2
Murphy Derris Dust	AA 29, CA 16
Murphy Fentro	AA 13
Murphy Gamma-BHC Dust	AA 14
Murphy Hormone Rooting Powder	KA 2
Murphy Kil-Ant	AA 21
Murphy Lawn Pest Killer	BA 1, BE 2
Murphy Lawn Weed Killer & Lawn Tonic	BC 7
Murphy Liquid Malathion	AA 18, CA 8
Murphy Malathion Dust	AA 18, CA 8
Murphy Mole Smokes	J 8
Murphy Mortegg	AC 8, BC 24, BD 13, EB 3
Murphy Path Weed Killer	EA 1
Murphy Permethrin Whitefly Smokes	CA 9
Murphy Pest & Disease Smokes	CC 2
Murphy Problem Weeds Killer	EA 5
Murphy Ready-to-Use Tumbleweed Sprayer	AD 7, EA 16
Murphy Slugit Liquid	F 4
Murphy Slugits	F 4
Murphy Sodium Chlorate	EA 18
Murphy Super Weedex	EA 7
Murphy Systemic Insecticide	AA 10
Murphy Traditional Copper Fungicide	AB 4, CB 3
Murphy Tumbleblite	AB 9
Murphy Tumblebug	AA 17, CA 7
Murphy Tumblemoss	BD 3
Murphy Tumbleweed	AD 7, EA 16
Murphy Tumbleweed Gel	AD 7, BC 22, EA 16
Murphy Weedex	AD 9, EA 17
New Formula SBK Brushwood Killer	EA 10
Nimrod T	AB 2
Nippon Ant & Crawling Insect Killer	GA 17
Nippon Ant Killer Liquid	AA 3, GA 4
No Weed	AD 8
Nobble Garden Pack	F 2
Notcutts Granular Lawn Feed & Weed	BC 2
Notcutts Lawn Sand	BD 12
Oak Lawnmaster Lawn Feed with Weedkiller	BC 4
Pathclear	EA 4
Payless Lawn Feed & Weed	BC 12
PBI Arbrex	AE 1
PBI Autumn & Winter Toplawn	BA 2, BE 3
PBI Boltac Greasebands	AA 16
PBI Bromophos	AA 5, CA 2

PBI Calomel Dust	AB 7
PBI Cheshunt Compound	AB 5, CB 4,
PBI Crop Saver	AA 19
PBI Fenitrothion	AA 13
PBI Hexyl	AC 6
PBI Kybosh	GA 16, GB 9
PBI Liquid Derris	AA 29, CA 16
PBI Malathion Greenfly Killer	AA 18, CA 8
PBI Pepper Dust	H 4
PBI Racumin Mouse Bait	J 6
PBI Racumin Rat Bait	J 6
PBI Slug Gard	F 5
PBI Slug Mini-Pellets	F 4
PBI Supercarb	AB 3, BB 2, CB 6
PBI Systhane	AB 8
PBI Toplawn	BC 4
PBI Velvas	BD 12
Pepper Dust	H 4
Picket	AA 20, CA 9
Plant Pins	D 3
Pocket Touchweeder	BC 13
Pokon Mildew Spray	AB 10, D 9
Prevent	GB 12
Proctors Lawn Weed & Feed	BC 12
Py Garden Insecticide	AA 25, CA 13
Py Powder	AA 25, CA 13, GA 20
Py Spray Garden Insect Killer	AA 25, CA 13, GA 20, GB 12
Raid Ant & Crawling Insect Killer	GA 2
Raid Fly & Wasp Killer	GB 2
Rapid	AA 22, CA 10
Rapid Aerosol	AA 22, CA 10
Ratak	J 7
Rentokil Alphakil	J 1
Rentokil Ant & Crawling Insect Killer	GA 12
Rentokil Ant & Insect Powder	AA 6, GA 6
Rentokil Ant Killer	AA 3, GA 4
Rentokil Biotrol Plus Outdoor Rat Killer	J 3
Rentokil Blackfly & Greenfly Killer	AA 26, CA 14
Rentokil Carpet Beetle Killer & Mothproofer	GC 2
Rentokil Exterior Mouldicide Tri-Spot	EB 1
Rentokil Flea Killer	GA 14
Rentokil Fly & Wasp Killer	GB 10
Rentokil Greenhouse & Garden Insect Killer	AA 26, CA 14
Rentokil Houseplant Insect Killer	D 10
Rentokil Insectrol	GA 9, GB 4
Rentokil Mouse Killer System	J 3
Rentokil Path & Patio Weedkiller	EA 2
Rentokil Rodine C Rat & Mouse Killer	J 3
Rentokil Wasp Nest Killer	AA 6
Root-Out	EA 8
Roseclear	AC 1

Sactif Flying Insect Killer	GB 10
Safers Fruit & Vegetable Insecticide	AA 12, CA 6
Safers Garden Fungicide	AB 11
Safers House Plant Insecticide	D 6
Safers Rose & Flower Insecticide	AA 12, CA 6
Savona	AA 12, CA 6
Scent-Off Buds	H 3
Scent-Off Pellets	H 3
Scoot	H 1
Scram	H 4
Secto Ant & Crawling Insect Lacquer	GA 8
Secto Aphid Killer	AA 9, CA 4
Secto Extra Strength Ant Killer Powder	AA 15, GA 14
Secto Flea Free Insecticidal Rug & Carpet Freshener	GA 15
Secto Flora Spray Systemic Insect Killer	D 5
Secto Fly Killer	GB 10
Secto Garden Powder	AC 4, CC 1
Secto Greenfly & Garden Insect Spray	AA 15
Secto Hormone Rooting Powder	KA 4
Secto House & Garden Powder	AA 15, GA 14
Secto Household Flea Killer	GA 11, GB 6
Secto Insect Killer Powder	AA 15, GA 14
Secto Kil-a-Line	GA 8
Secto Moth Proofer	GC 1
Secto Rapid Action Flykiller Liquid	GB 7
Secto Rose & Flower Spray	AC 4, CC 1
Secto Slow Release Flykiller Kitchen Size	GB 5
Secto Slug Kil Pellets	F 4
Secto Systemic Garden Insect Killer Concentrate	AA 11, CA 5
Secto Wasp Killer Aerosol	AA 15
Sectovap Flykiller Lantern Living Room Size	GB 5
Sectovap Greenhouse Pest Killer	CA 3
Sectovap Moth Killer	GB 5
Sectovap New Minispace	GB 5
Septico Slug Killer	F 1
Sergeants Rug Patrol	GA 18
Slug & Snail Killer Pellets	F 4
Snail Control	F 3
Sodium Chlorate	EA 18
Soil Insecticide Powder	AA 14
Sorexa CD Mouse Killer	J 4
Spraydex General Purpose Fungicide	AB 5, CB 4
Spraydex Greenfly Killer	AA 2
Spraydex Houseplant Spray	D 2, GA 3
Spraydex Insect Killer	GA 3
Spraydex Lawn Spot Weeder	BC 11
Spring Spray	AA 5
Stay Off	H 1
Stop-Gro G8	KB 2

Sulphur Candles	CD 3
Sybol	AA 23, BA 3, CA 11
Sybol Aerosol	AA 24, CA 12
Sybol Dust	AA 23
Synchemicals Couch & Grass Killer	AD 3, EA 11
Synchemicals House Plant Pest Killer	D 10
Synchemicals Rooting Powder	KA 2
Synchemicals Tomato Setting Spray	KC 1
Systhane	AB 8
Tar Oil Winter Wash	AC 8
Tenax Wax	AE 3
Tox Exterminating Fly Spray	GB 8
Trappit Codling Moth Traps	KD 3
Triple Action Grasshopper	BC 5, BD 5
Ultrasect Strip	GB 5
Vapona Ant & Crawling Insect Killer	GA 3
Vapona Ant & Crawling Insect Powder	GA 15
Vapona Ant & Crawling Insect Spray	GA 1
Vapona Ant Pen	GA 7
Vapona Fly Killer	CA 3, GB 5
Vapona Fly Killer Aerosol	GB 3
Vapona Fly Pen	GA 7
Vapona Moth Killer	GB 5
Vapona Moth Proofer Aerosol	GC 3
Vapona Small Space Fly Killer	GB 5
Verdone 2	BC 11
Verdone 2 Spot Weeder	BC 11
Vitax Lawn Sand	BD 12
Vitax Weed'N'Feed Extra	BC 10, BD 6
Warfarin 0.5% Concentrate	J 9
Warfarin Ready Mixed Bait	J 9
Wasp Exterminator	AA 29
Waspend	GA 19, GB 11
Weed Gun for Lawns	BC 3
Weedol	AD 6, EA 14
Wilko Lawn Feed'N'Weed	BC 12
Wilko Lawn Food With Weedkiller	BC 12
Wilko Lawn Sand	BD 12
Wilko Soluble Lawn Food & Weedkiller	BC 20
6X Slug Killer	F 1
Yellow Sulphur	AB 11
Yellow Sulphur Powder	AB 11

Appendix 1

List of firms and addresses

Ace: Ace Chemicals Ltd.
Loanwath Road
Gretna
Dumfriess. CA6 5ES
(0461) 37572

Agralan: Agralan
The Old Brickyard
Ashton Keynes
Swindon
Wilts. SN6 6QR
(0285) 860015

Agrichem: Agrichem Ltd.
Padholme Road
Peterborough
Cambs. PE1 5XL
(0733) 47881

Agropharm: Agropharm Ltd.
Buckingham House
Church Road
Penn
High Wycombe
Bucks. HP10 8LN
(0494) 814619

Aitken: R. Aitken
123 Harmony Road
Govan
Glasgow GS1 3NB
041-440 0033

Arable & Bulb:
    Arable & Bulb Chemicals Ltd.
Main Road
Butterwick
Boston
Lincs. PE22 0JW
(0205) 760479

Armillatox: Armillatox Ltd.
44 Town Street
Duffield
Derby DE6 4GH
(0332) 841151

ASDA: ASDA Stores Ltd.
ASDA House
South Bank
Gt. Wilson Street
Leeds LS11 5AD
(0532) 435435

Ashlade:
    Ashlade Formulations Ltd.
Ness Road
Slade Green
Erith
Kent DA8 2LD
(0322) 331671

Atlas: Atlas Interlates Ltd.
PO Box 38
Low Moor
Bradford
W. Yorks. BD12 0JZ
(0274) 671267

B&Q: B&Q Ltd.
Portswood House
1 Hampshire Corporate Park
Chandlers Ford
Eastleigh
Hants. SO5 3YX
(0703) 620212

B H & B:
    Battle, Hayward & Bower Ltd.
Victoria Chemical Works
Crofton Drive
Allenby Road Industrial Estate
Lincoln LN3 4NP
(0522) 29206

Boots: The Boots Company plc.
Merchandise Technical Services
Nottingham NG2 3AA
(0602) 866671

Chipman: Chipman Ltd.
Horsham
Sussex RH12 2NR
(0403) 60341

Chrysal: Chrysal Ltd.
1 Whitehall Place
Wallington
Surrey SM6 0TT
01-647 4797

Ciba: Ciba-Geigy Agrochemicals
Whittlesford
Cambridge CB2 4QT
(0223) 833621

Cooke: Cookes Chemicals
Llanbedr
Gwynnedd
(034 123) 301

Cramphorn: Cramphorn plc.
Cuton Mill
Chelmsford
Essex CM2 6PD
(0245) 466221

Dax: Dax Products Ltd.
76 Cyprus Road
Nottingham NG3 5ED
(0602) 42334

De Witt: E C De Witt & Co. Ltd.
Tudor Road
Manor Park
Runcorn
Cheshire WA7 1SZ
(0928) 581237

Doff: Doff Portland Ltd.
Bolsover Street
Hucknall
Nottingham NG15 7TY
(0602) 632842

Domestic Fillers:
  Domestic Fillers Ltd.
10 Thames Road
Barking
Essex IG11 0HU
01-594 2236

Elliott: Thomas Elliott Ltd.
Hast Hill
Hayes
Bromley
Kent BR2 7RJ
01-462 1207

English Woodlands:
  English Woodlands Ltd.
Graffham
Petworth
Sussex GU28 0LR
(079 86) 574

Fertosan: Fertosan Products
  (Wirral) Ltd.
2 Holborn Square
Birkenhead
Merseyside L41 9HQ
051-647 5809

Fieldspray: Fieldspray Division
Nilco Chemical Co. Ltd.
Stewart Road
Kingsland Industrial Park
Basingstoke
Hants. RG24 0GX
(0256) 474661

Fisons: Fisons plc.
Horticulture Division
Paper Mill Lane
Bramford
Ipswich
Suffolk IP8 4BZ
(0473) 830492

Ford Smith: Ford Smith & Co. Ltd.
Lyndean Industrial Estate
Felixstowe Road
Abbey Wood
London SE2 9SG
01-310 8127

Garotta: Garotta Products Ltd.
Firth Road
Lincoln LN6 7AH
(0522) 537561

Geeco: Geeco Division
Mc Kechnie Consumer Products Ltd.
Gore Road Industrial Estate
New Milton
Hants. BH25 6SE
(0425) 614600

Gem: Gem Gardening
Joseph Metcalf Ltd.
Brookside Lane
Oswaldtwistle
Accrington BB5 3NY
(0254) 393321

Gerhardt: Gerhardt
    Pharmaceuticals Ltd.
Thornton House
Hook Road
Surbiton
Surrey KT6 5AR
01-397 9418

Get-Off-My-Garden:
    Get-Off-My-Garden Ltd.
The Stables
Sanquhar House
Sanquhar
Dumfries DG4 6JL
(0659) 50141

Growing Success: Growing
    Success Organics Ltd.
South Newton
Salisbury
Wilts.

HDRA: Henry Doubleday
    Research Association
Ryton-on-Dunsmore
Coventry CV8 3LG
(0203) 303517

Humber: Humber Fertilisers plc.
PO Box 57
Stoneferry
Hull HU8 8DQ
(0482) 20458

Hurrans: Hurrans Garden Centres
68 St. John's Avenue
Churchdown
Glos. GL3 2BX
(0452) 712232

ICI: ICI Garden Products
Woolmead House East
Woolmead Walk
Farnham
Surrey GU9 7UB
(0252) 303517

Interpet: Interpet Ltd.
Vincent Lane
Dorking
Surrey RH4 3YX
(0306) 881033

Jeyes: Jeyes Ltd.
Brunel Way
Thetford
Norwich
(0842) 754567

Johnson's Vet.: Johnson's
    Veterinary Products Ltd.
5 Reddicap Trading Estate
Coleshill Road
Sutton Coldfield
W. Midlands B75 7DF
021-378 1684

Johnson Wax: Johnson Wax Ltd.
Frimley Green
Camberley
Surrey GU16 5AJ
(0276) 63456

Keen: Keen (World Marketing) Ltd.
Ridgeway
Iver
Bucks. SL0 9JQ
(0753) 652406

Kent Country:
    Kent Country Nurseries
Challock
Nr. Ashford
Kent TN25 4DG
(023 374) 256

Koppert: Koppert (UK) Ltd.
PO Box 43
Tunbridge Wells
Kent TN2 5BX
(0892) 36807

Lever: Lever Industrial Ltd.
PO Box 100
Runcorn
Cheshire WA7 3JZ
(0928) 719000

May & Baker:
    May & Baker Garden Care
Fyfield Road
Ongar
Essex CM5 0HW
(0277) 362127

Maxicrop:
    Maxicrop International Ltd.
Bridge House
97–101 High Street
Tonbridge
Kent TN9 1DR
(0732) 366710

Mill: Mill (Horticultural) Ltd.
Roundhead Road
Newton Abbott
Devon
(0626) 331177

Monsanto:
    Monsanto Agricultural Co.
Thames Tower
Burleys Way
Leics. LE1 3TP
(0533) 620864

Napa: Napa Products Ltd.
Barmston House
Barmston Road
Beverley
E. Yorks. HU17 0LA
(0482) 871479

Nicholas: Ashe Consumer
    Products Ltd.
Ashetree Works
Kingston Road
Leatherhead
Surrey KT22 7JZ
(0372) 376151

Notcutt's: Notcutt's Garden
    Centres Ltd.
Ipswich Road
Woodbridge
Suffolk IP12 4AF
(039 43) 3344

Oak: Oak Horticulture
68 Carlton Road
Worksop
Notts. S80 1DY
(0909) 500777

Organic Concentrates:
    Organic Concentrates Ltd.
3 Broadway Court
Chesham
Bucks. HP5 1EN
(0494) 792229

PBI: Pan Brittanica Industries Ltd.
Brittanica House
Waltham Cross
Herts. EN8 7DY
(0992) 23691

Phostrogen: Phostrogen Ltd.
Corwen
Clwyd LL21 0EE
(0490) 2662

Proctor: H & T Proctor
Cole Road
Off Feeder Road
Bristol BS22 0UG
(0272) 774521

**Reckitt: Reckitt Household &
  Toiletry Products**
Reckitt House
Stoneferry Road
Hull HU8 8DD
(0482) 223141

Rentokil: Rentokil Ltd.
Felcourt
East Grinstead
W. Sussex RH19 2JY
(0342) 833022

Robins: A H Robins Co. Ltd.
Consumer Products Division
Sussex Manor Business Park
Gatwick Road
Crawley
W. Sussex RH10 2NH
(0293) 560161

**Rohm & Haas:
  Rohm & Haas (UK) Ltd.**
Lennig House
2 Masons Avenue
Croydon
Surrey CR9 3NB
01-686 8844

Secto: Secto Company Ltd.
Carlinghurst Road
Blackburn
Lancs. BB2 1PW
(0254) 61632

Septico: Septico Ltd.
184 Henwood Road
Tettenhull
Wolverhampton
W. Midlands
(0902) 752242

**Sinclair: Sinclair Horticulture &
  Leisure Ltd.**
Firth Road
Lincoln LN6 7AH
(0522) 537561

Sorex: Sorex Ltd.
St. Michaels Industrial Estate
Hale Road
Widnes
Cheshire WA8 8TJ
051-420 715

**Sphere: Sphere Laboratories
  (London) Ltd.**
The Yews
Main Street
Chilton
Oxford OX11 0RZ
(0235) 833896

Spraydex: Spraydex Ltd.
Moreton Avenue
Wallingford
Oxford OX10 9DE
(0491) 25251

Synchemicals: Synchemicals Ltd.
Owen Street
Coalville
Leics. LE6 2DE
(0530) 510060

Vitax: Vitax Ltd.
Selby Place
Stanley Industrial Estate
Skelmersdale
Lancs. WN8 8EF
(0695) 51834

**Wallace, Cameron:
  Wallace, Cameron & Co. Ltd.**
303 Drakemire Drive
Glasgow G45 9SU
041-634 6881